CH PLANTING
OUR FUTURE HOPE

CHARLIE CLEVERLY

Scripture Union
130 City Road, London EC1V 2NJ

For John Reeves, who never tires of telling others about the unsearchable riches of Christ.

First published 1991.

British Library CIP Data
Cleverly, Charlie
Church planting.
1. Great Britain. New churches. Development
I. Title
254.10941

ISBN 0 86201 571 5

Credits

Two quotations from the work of T S Eliot are reprinted by permission of Faber and Faber Ltd from *Collected Poems 1909–1962* by T S Eliot. The newspaper story with which chapter 2 opens appeared in *The Times* 21 August 1985 and is copyright © Times Newspapers Ltd 1985. It is reprinted with permission. The newspaper story in chapter 5 is copyright © The Sunday Telegraph Limited, London and is used with permission. The prophecy quoted in chapter 8 is from *Prophecy*, copyright © 1976 Bruce Yocum, published by Servant Publications, Box 8617, Ann Arbor, Michigan 48107. It is used with permission. The excerpt from *Life Together* by Dietrich Bonhoeffer in chapter 11 is copyright © 1954 Harper and Row Publishers, Inc. It is reprinted by permission of HarperCollins Publishers. 'My Parents', quoted in chapter 9, is taken from *Clearing Away the Rubbish*, © 1988 Adrian Plass, and is reprinted by permission of Monarch Publications Ltd, 1 St Anne's Road, Eastbourne, BN21 3UN. The song There's another kind of famine by John Clarke and Philip Glassborow, quoted in chapter 10, is copyright © 1988 Thankyou Music, P O Box 75, Eastbourne, East Sussex, BN23 6NW, UK. It is used with permission. Extracts from the Book of Common Prayer of 1662, the rights in which are vested in the Crown in perpetuity within the United Kingdom, are reproduced in chapter 5 and at the beginning of chapter 13 by permission of the Crown's patentee, Cambridge University Press.

The cartoons in this book originally appeared in *Leadership*. Those on pages, 38, 161 and 167 are by Jim Paillot and are the copyright of *Leadership* magazine. The cartoon on page 68 is by Doug Hall. That on page 85 is by Erik Johnson. That on page 109 is by Eddie Eddings. The cartoon on page 115 is by Dan Pegoda (concept: Wendell W Simons) and is the copyright of *Leadership* magazine.

The cover design and artwork are by Adept Design.

Scripture quotation in this publication are from the Holy Bible, New International Version, Copyright © 1973, 1978, 1984 International Bible Society. Published by Hodder and Stoughton.

Phototypeset by Input Typesetting Ltd, London.

Printed and bound in Great Britain by Cox and Wyman Ltd, Reading.

Contents

Foreword		5
Acknowledgements		7
1	Swept along by God	9
2	Why plant churches today?	13
3	Getting moving	27
4	Some current initiatives in church planting	42
5	One a month	58
6	'Give me a hundred men . . .'	75
7	Finding the missing jewel	89
8	Hearing the voice of the Lord	105
9	All you need is love	118
10	Another kind of famine	131
11	'As each part does its work . . .'	142
12	Troubleshooting	155
13	Fighting the principalities and powers	171
14	Heart cry for revival	181
Appendix		184
Notes		187

Foreword

It is a privilege to write a foreword to Charlie Cleverly's necessary and timely book on church planting.

There are few denominations now who would resist as unnecessary the planting of new congregations of Christians. Our rapidly changing and mobile society has produced vast tracts of unevangelised peoples – in and out of the city. It is now widely recognised by Christians around the world that the most effective way to evangelise, or re-evangelise, a society is by planting churches. Past complacency, small mindedness, or a life-style which is designed for preserving 'my kingdom' rather than promoting God's, are collapsing before the necessity to obey the Lord in the great commission. The best way for men and women to be confronted with Christ's claims is to see on their own doorstep a relevant body of believers worshipping and sharing in their common life in Jesus. New churches achieve this end. They are the fastest way of evangelising in depth, since church bodies reproduce 'after their kind' more bodies of Christians. These fresh congregations can be relevant to the structure and the culture of the society in which they are planted without the tedious business of undoing the past and rolling away what might be called 'the reproach of Egypt' which hangs around so many buildings or so many more traditional structures often inherited from a not too healthy past.

Charlie is, as he will tell us, an Anglican clergyman. As such he is involved in a parish system which is rightly aimed to cover the whole territory of the United Kingdom. However, he will argue that there is still 'much land to possess' and that the current parish system is inadequate. His challenge to us to church plant is perceptive, practical and persuasive. The presentation of different models, rather than one only as a definitive blueprint, makes the book widely useful. His description of our own model in Ichthus, where we have planted, to date, 32 congregations in London, plus a few abroad, is very generous. His humility of mind and lack of partisan spirit are commendable and, no doubt, contributory to the effectiveness of his own ministry in the parish of Cranham, Essex.

If this book could help in stimulating a church planting wave through the country, so that in every thousand people there arose a viable, living congregation of Christians, Charlie Cleverly and I would be well pleased. And so – I humbly believe – would our Saviour.

Roger Forster

Acknowledgements

My dear wife Annie is the one whom I wish to thank publicly for her enthusiasm for this book and her help in encouraging the discipline needed to write it. The first thing I have to thank her for is introducing me to Jesus Christ. Ever since then it has been an increasing joy to be together in serving him: this book is an expression of our life together. So thank you, darling! Thanks also to Hannah, Alice, Jack and Jemimah who are a delight and have put up with Dad's absence with great good humour.

I'm grateful to David Pytches and Roger Forster for their enthusiasm for this project and helpful comments on the manuscript, but above all for their fearless and tireless example in pressing for the growth of the church.

Friends at home have been such an encouragement. Fellow staff members John Guest, Peter Blows, Dick Saunders and Bill Picknell have shown great encouragment when it was most needed and have helped in taking different tasks. Thanks also are due to our elders for their understanding and vision.

At Scripture Union my editor, Campbell Grant, has been extemely helpful and thoughtful in different kinds of clear advice which has shaped the book. Thank you, Jane Bejon, for typing some initial chapters. But most of all – in terms of tireless, accurate typing and organising – I'm grateful to Frances Simmonds, known affectionately among us as St Frances of Cranham!

1

Swept along by God

With the drawing of this Love and the voice of this Calling
We shall not cease from exploration
And the end of all our exploring
Will be to arrive where we started
And know the place for the first time.

T S Eliot

'Hartmut Kopsch has been on the phone,' said my wife Annie, 'about a job in Cranham. I don't think I want to go.' Hartmut, a friend from Trinity College, Bristol, a gifted personal evangelist and now a curate, was ringing to see if we would go and work with him in a small commuter suburb of Upminster in Essex.

In fact, neither of us wanted to go to Cranham – which we thought would be within sniffing distance of the Dartford Tunnel and all that was drab and deadly about south-east England. I was working on a street theatre mission in Bristol when the call came, getting in at 1.00 am after doing gospel presentations in the clubs and discotheques at night. I remember one particularly seedy dive called the Dugout which we left with our clothes reeking of marijuana and our ears ringing with reggae but our hearts full of joy for the privilege of gaining a hearing for Christ. I suppose we thought, to our shame, that commuter land would be hard to live with after the beauty and breadth of Bristol.

It wasn't until a week later that I was able to ring John Reeves, vicar of St Luke's, Cranham, who later said that he was intrigued from the word go by the strange activities we were involved with when he first contacted us. For myself, I was hooked by John's radical zeal to see the gospel go out to all. Later on, whenever our friends on a visit happened to meet him they would ask: 'Is he really a vicar?' Partly because he seemed to have the secret of eternal youth; but mainly because, unlike too many, he was into mission and not maintenance.

Eight years ago we began work in St Luke's, Cranham where the church was growing and several people were coming to Christ. We soon found that, though the surroundings were drab, the people were alive with love for God and love for us. The first thing we had to do was to repent of our childish attitude. Alongside the usual duties of a curate, I worked as leader of a faith sharing team which was sent out to many parishes leading weekends of renewal and weeks of mission. Soon after I arrived, with the parish church nearly full (it seats about 250), Hartmut took a team of twelve out from the church to form a new congregation in a disused Brethren hall given to us free of charge. St Luke's spent £40,000 on the building, gave away one of its full-time staff and several of its members and the new church began, slowly but surely, to grow.

Then, just over two years later, John announced at the AGM (which we use as an opportunity to set spiritual and practical goals for the year to come) that he felt the time had come for church number three. He asked those interested or intrigued by the idea to pray as to whether God might be calling them personally to this work. I'll write more about testing the call to such work, but within a few months we gave up our travelling ministry and took a team of sixteen adults plus their children out of St Luke's and began Cranham Community Church. After a violent struggle this grew to a membership of around a hundred within three years. During these months we found that we were part of what amounts to a movement in Britain today, with churches springing up everywhere.

The numbers mentioned above are very small, but if they were to be multiplied hundreds and hundreds of times across the nation they would become enormous. In the last few years it has become clear that many other churches are working in this way in every denomination. My view is that this is the work of the Holy Spirit, planting hundreds of small, vital congregations in schools, pubs, gyms; wherever a hall can be hired. David Pawson once said: 'My ambition is to find out what God is doing and join in.' It has been a privilege to 'join in' in Cranham in a very small way with what God is doing.

But if it is work in which we can join, the question needs to be asked: will we respond decisively? David Watson used to say: 'He who would work with the Holy Spirit must learn to move fast.' But will churches, and even denominations, get involved in this without another decade of delays? Roy Pointer, after extensive research for the Bible Society, commented in 1984:

> Although we are in a missionary situation very few plans for evangelism and church planting are being drawn up by British denominations.
>
> God is a planner and he has plans for the British Isles. Therefore we have to discover his plans and act accordingly. The great receptivity to the Good News in the United Kingdom today encourages me to believe that a harvest is prepared and yet few bold, denominational plans exist for evangelism and growth. Instead I hear of plans for decline, closure and redundancy. There are at least 36 million people to be won for Christ, but where are the plans drawn up in response to the challenge and opportunity?
>
> Bold plans consistent with God's plans are required and they should be drawn up without delay. I personally

believe that the planting of thousands of new churches (communities of believers) is consistent with God's plans for the United Kingdom today.[1]

We shall see that the position has changed slightly, but encouragingly, since this challenge was given.

My own burden in writing this book is that as wide a circle of believers as possible consider biblical and practical principles for church planting that will enable us to promote and plan for growth more effectively. But first we need to ask: is church planting an effective means to the growth of the church? We need to answer the question: why plant churches today?

2

Why plant churches today?

O England, full of sin, but most of sloth;
Spit out thy phlegm, and fill thy breast with glory.

George Herbert

I still remember the strong emotions aroused in me when I read the following news report in my morning paper.

Child locked in house with dead parents

A girl, aged two, who was locked in her home for nearly 24 hours with the bodies of her dead parents was being looked after by relatives yesterday.

The mother, aged 22, of Wolverhampton, had been stabbed to death and her husband, aged 30, was hanging by an electric cable from a loft beam.

Neighbours called the police after the little girl whispered through the letterbox: 'My mummy and daddy are asleep.'

One might also whisper, 'The church is asleep!' while such scenes of despair occur each week in our nation. And yet how many tragic cases of hopelessness in families and amongst children are there which never reach our newspapers? Behind one door in three in each street or high rise there is a family affected by the confusion of divorce, to name just one cause for distress. The church is the channel chosen and appointed by God to bring hope to the hopeless – and yet often the church is not present in the very place where she is needed most.

Expresses love for the lost

Although many towns and housing estates are served by live and dynamic churches, many are not, and even within a small community of 12,000 like ours in Cranham, there can still be whole estates from which only a handful of people are Christians. If this is so, then the church may begin to experience something of the grief of Jesus going 'through all the towns and villages' and being filled with compassion because the crowds 'were harrassed and helpless, like sheep without a shepherd'. In his concern, Jesus pleads for workers to be sent out into the harvest field.

At the time of writing we are considering one particular estate. We have begun to ask the Lord and ask the church to send out workers into this particular harvest field with the aim of finding out what needs there are in the area, offering practical help from house to house and seeing who would like to consider following Jesus. Then we envisage starting a housegroup on the estate, and then a monthly family service, and in the end a church. At present we have no committed team, no leaders, and certainly no building, but we do have a clear conviction that this is the next step in church planting for us to take.

The first great motive for planting churches today is that we might reach the lost. Every church planting endeavour must be tested by this question: will those outside the kingdom be helped to enter the kingdom through this new church? Will those who are without hope and without God in the world have more chance of finding hope if we start this new church? If we cannot answer, 'Yes this is our motive,' then all the other good pragmatic reasons for church planting are irrelevant. But if we can say Yes to this acid test, then we will find several other reasons for planting churches today which will spur us on to do so. Below I have detailed, first, some of the more pressing practical reasons for church planting today, followed by a more developed rationale for the necessity of such a strategy.

Breaks through prejudice

I recently heard of a family who invited to church some friends who were staying with them for the weekend. Reluctantly they agreed to go. All went well for the outing until at one particularly reverent moment, the young son of the party stood on his seat and inquired with a loud voice: 'Dad, where are all the hypocrites?' Hilarity and consternation ensued.

One might think that with the nation stuffed full of church buildings, few of which are stuffed full of people, the last thing needed is to plant new ones. However, people have often decided against the older churches because of past experiences which have led them to conclude: 'The church is full of hypocrites!' They have no intention of moving house and the neighbourhood is well served by the 'hypocritical church' against which they are irrevocably prejudiced. How in this context are they to be drawn back to Jesus' people? Our experience has been that to create a new expression of the body of Christ has been to create a new possibility of conversion for many such people. This has been the case even though the new church has been conceived and brought into being by the hypocrites themselves! The ability of a new church to break through prejudice is a second, more pragmatic reason for planting churches today.

Breaks with offputting traditions

I was brought up in liberal Anglicanism and lapsed into unbelief and active opposition before being converted in an evangelical Anglican church at the age of twenty-four. I well remember going as a new convert into a Baptist church for the first time: how strange I found that row of five deacons' chairs which dominated the scene, and even stranger the little cups for communion. Had it been the other way round, and I was experiencing an Anglican church for the first time, the shock might have been even greater. In the church where I was converted, the service began with a muffled announcement from the back, followed by a lengthy hymn during which thirty men and women in long blue dresses, white nightshirts and yellowing ruffs walked up and down the various corridors in the building singing at the top of their voices. As they came close we watched as they demonstrated the subtle science of reading the often obscure words of the hymn and seeing where they were going at the same time.

I often wonder just how extraordinary some of our customs must appear to those who have no experience of churchgoing. And at the end of the twentieth century, it is the unchurched who make up the vast, tens of millions strong majority of the population. The potentially off-putting nature of these expressions of church life to the new convert are taken for granted by C S Lewis in *The Screwtape Letters*. In this extract the senior devil instructs his nephew to use them as a tactic in subverting the progress of the new believer:

> One of the greatest allies at present is the church itself. Do not misunderstand me. I do not mean the church as we see her spread out through all time and space and rooted in eternity, terrible as an army with banners. That, I confess, is a spectacle which makes our boldest tempters uneasy but fortunately it is quite invisible to these humans. All your patient sees is the half-finished sham Gothic erection on the new building estate. When he goes inside, he sees the local grocer with a rather oily expression on his face bustling up to offer him one shiny little book containing a liturgy which neither of them understands, and one shabby little book containing corrupt texts of a number of religious lyrics, mostly bad, and in very small print.

So a third reason for church planting is that, when a new

church starts, it has a golden opportunity not to obscure the gospel in its public meetings with cultural clutter from another generation. For us, even as an Anglican church, it has been important not to wear robes in these new churches. The community church started in a home and to wear them would have been distinctly odd. Similarly, it seemed a natural thing when we began to have a coffee break in the middle of the service. There is provision for this in the Anglican Alternative Service Book of course under the heading of The Peace! Similarly, we need to ask: what kind of music is most easily understood by the visitor? In our society today the use of an organ is a rarified form of museum culture, whereas guitars and synthesisers are heard and seen every day on television. For the music to be led by a worship band seems to me to be more appropriate to our culture.

These minor changes in style are all designed to make the unchurched newcomer feel that when he visits the church he is not visiting another planet. One new church in America called its sanctuary The Living Room, so keen was it to remain normal. If all can be made relatively understandable to newcomers, then they will be better disposed to listening to the word of God preached with conviction, which the Bible says contains the seed of life to those who are otherwise perishing. We need to admit that for many older churches it takes much longer to change and also that a more traditional style can be helpful to many in finding Christ personally and following him radically. But the brand new church can press the question: what at this time is most pleasing to God and most helpful to the completely unchurched outsider?

Each church needs to examine the traditions which inevitably grow up around its worship to see what should be discarded as being a barrier to the one seeking God. Jesus chucked out the rubbish from the temple and swept away some of the traditions that had grown up over the years, insisting that his house become again a house of prayer for all nations. Each church needs to ask: is ours a community where all kinds of people can come into an intimate relationship with God? Is it a house of prayer or is it unhelpfully cluttered? The new congregation has a heaven sent opportunity to begin again to do all it can in public worship to present Christ in such a way that those who don't know him can find him.

Brings faster growth

Britain's church life has been compared not to a virgin landscape but to a garden which has been planted already. 'Church planting in Britain must be done in a densely packed denominational shrubbery,' comments veteran missionary Michael Griffiths.[1] But even in a dense garden, plants grow old and die and cuttings need to be taken. Eventually, if given enough care and space, the new cuttings will grow stronger and larger than the mother plant herself. So a fourth reason for planting new churches is that a young and vibrant expression of church life is encouraged which can often grow faster than the older churches. Lest this be seen as potentially threatening, it is important for the mother church to see this as her own growth. It is through church planting that the mother church can grow most quickly. When a church is in her infancy there will be the most visible signs of growth, as with a child. It is of course important that growth in size be linked to growth in maturity, otherwise we may simply see the fulfilment of Jesus' warning about the seed sown on the rock, which shoots up fast but withers because its roots are not deep enough. Here it is vital to complement the evangelistic enthusiasm with the gifts of pastor and teacher and to lay good foundations of a radical biblical understanding of the church at the same time as pressing on in evangelism. We shall examine in later chapters exactly what these foundations for a new church should be.

Expands a full church

Perhaps the most pressing reason for planting a new church is when the mother church is full. We believe that in the present climate of great openness to the gospel and of great need in people's broken lives, it is a godly thing to expect growth and to plant accordingly.

Our experience, even in the Church of England, is that it is not a foolhardy thing to plan to double the numbers in a local church over a period of two or three years. But if a church is comfortably full on Sunday mornings, how can it possibly double in size? There are three possibilities: one is to have a repeat morning service, the second is to build a bigger building and the third and most flexible option is to plant a new church or churches.

When I arrived in Cranham the church was not packed but was getting full on Sunday mornings. I was dismayed when I woke up to the fact that the plan was not to wait or extend the building but to send twenty people and their children away to start another church. I thought it foolhardy and told my colleague John so. He replied that it did seem strange to him too, but that at every stage God – as far as they could discern – had opened the way to do this. And so it was that plans went ahead. On the very Sunday that the new church opened we looked in vain for the empty seats in St Luke's: it seemed that God had given to us at the mother church a new group of people who had either moved into the area or who were to be converted and we saw the truth of the saying: 'Give and it will be given to you, pressed down and running over.' If we wanted now to bring our congregations together on Sunday morning it would be completely impossible in the original building; in fact we would fill it twice over.

Promotes 'natural growth'

The very day that we began to meet in the community centre where we are based, three mothers with their children began to attend. I had never met any of them before. Later on, when we distributed publicity or went door to door visiting, we never failed to draw at least one family to come and see this new thing which had come to pass. When we went visiting we simply wanted to give information and an invitation. Our remarks went like this: 'Hello, we are from St Luke's Church in Front Lane, do you know it? Yes? Well, we want to let you know that a new church is opening just down the road from you. It's going to be called Cranham Community Church. Have you seen this publicity which should have been put through your door? No? Here is a card which explains what we're doing. St Luke's is pretty full on Sundays now, so a whole group of us led by the Revd Charlie Cleverly are starting a new church with a Family Service this Sunday morning; would you be interested in coming?' We have found that it is good to be factual and helpful on these occasions and that always one or two who live opposite, or round the corner or who know the building have been drawn in. There will usually be those who are quite well disposed towards the church but who are drifting. Some may be converted and disillusioned, others will be unconverted but believing or searching people. When you start a new church, if you begin informatively you promote healthy natural growth among these people.

Promotes growth among Christians who go

I asked one member of a church planting team to look back on the experience. He said:

> When I first started with the team at Moor Lane my particular responsibility was for the children's talks. I had never done anything like that in my life, but I found that having to do it was in the end very exciting because you have to rely on the Lord and he supplies help in unforgettable ways. So personal growth at that time was in high leaps forward rather than in little trickles.

Such testimonies could be repeated over and over again as team members have had to take the lead in new areas they have found quite frightening. There is nothing wrong with such fear if it leads a Christian to cry out in weakness to God and exercise faith. It is almost a truism to say that the great danger for Christians is to become settlers and no longer to do anything that requires any risk. By contrast, Jesus called us to be constantly on the move, moving as pioneers into new situations in which we have to rely on God. Nothing I have experienced illustrates this quite like church planting because of the inherent risk of failure. When a team goes to a new area to start a new church, the fact is that they may fail, and the temptation is to fear that if they fail they will lose face. Therefore, it is certainly more comfortable to remain in the security of stable established church life. The Christian may be in a church which has been together for several hundred years, and so he knows there is a certain likelihood of it still being together next year! The church planting team have no such guarantees, and I for one have on occasions at the beginning wondered whether this team would still be together next week let alone next year. But such risks press one to go back to God who has called us and to rely on him, and this is so healthy for all Christians.

A second aspect of growth we discovered was that in joining a church planting team there is a fresh opportunity to discover the joy of adopting some of the lifestyle to which Jesus called us. This is particularly true of unity. Jesus prayed that we might be one as he and the Father are one. The earliest church in Jerusalem were able after the miracle of Pentecost to be 'one in heart and mind'. Yet in many older churches, which have known argument and misunderstanding, this has sadly been lost. As we start afresh to build a new church, we have a heaven sent opportunity to try again for this possibility of godly unity which, if we let it, will be so powerful in persuading the world of the divinity of Jesus. We will return to this foundation of church life in a later chapter, but it starts as the new team assembles, absolutely united in one goal, namely to win the lost and build a new church together. United in one goal, as perhaps never before in their Christian life, they will experience violent attack from without and within, and have to forgive each other seventy times seven, but will certainly grow in love for each other. With this love will come joy that such communality of life is after all possible and we can declare with David:

> How good and pleasant it is
> when brothers live together in unity!
> There the LORD bestows his blessing . . . (Psalm 133:1,3).

Promotes growth among Christians who stay

> I need help from you now. Charlie and his team have now gone. That is the reality. Last week they were here; now they have gone and they are not coming back. So I need your help first in prayer before the morning service. Who will come at 9.45 and pray?

When a sizeable group is commissioned and sent out from a church large gaps remain. This prayer alert called several together who had not previously seen it as their responsibility. In the mother church gaps may be left in all departments from Sunday Schools to sweeping up to speaking in tongues and interpreting. The group who came with me had in many cases exercised certain spiritual gifts in public worship and our going was a challenge to others to grow into these areas. Those who were quite recently converted began to take responsibility in different areas in which they had not seen a need prior to our departure. Those who had perhaps drawn back after much involvement came out of retirement to lead the church more effectively than ever before. And so in the mother church, there is a call to be pioneers again in new areas, and not to settle back, and this leads to growth in faith as people learn to call out to God again.

Biblical bedrock

We have looked at eight practical reasons for church planting today. But does it have a biblical basis? I believe it has.

Pioneers or settlers?
The call to move on was given by the Lord Jesus himself when he ordered his friends to 'Go!' It was not a command to stay put, but to go and make disciples of all the nations. It was of course so important that it was recorded by the gospel writers no less than five times. The epistles similarly exhort us to understand that to live as a Christian is to enter a life of change. The graffito which contradictorily proclaims, 'CONSTANT CHANGE IS HERE TO STAY', is true for the Christian. 'For here we do not have an enduring city, but we are looking for the city that is to come,' says the writer to the Hebrews. He exhorts us to remember the virtue of Abraham who left the stability of Ur of the Chaldees and obeyed God and went and 'made his home in the promised land like a stranger in a foreign country; he lived in tents.'

Often a new group of pioneers will consciously prefer to dwell in the 'tent' of rented accommodation. There is much that can be said about the advantages of such a strategy, which is flexible and which can penetrate secular buildings with the salt of the gospel touching the lives of many who otherwise have no contact with the church. We shall say more of this in another chapter, but Eileen Vincent emphasises this idea of the need to move on as she reflects on the church planting ministry:

> It seems that if a work is to continue to grow rather than to 'consolidate' (a word not found in my Bible!) the people need to be progressively taken forward from goal to goal. Once a target is attained – a building filled, new housegroups established – it is time to move on, time to present the next challenge. Too easily we stand still and pat ourselves on the back; before long we are losing ground.[2]

Planting new churches is one clear way of gaining ground for the kingdom of God. It is a way the Holy Spirit is using across the nation and across the denominations.

Matches the biblical mandate

Jesus' great commission was to go into all the world to make disciples. The **church** is the agency designed by God for causing those disciples to grow. When we ask how it was, after initial preaching, that people were won for Christ in Corinth, Ephesus, Rome, Thessalonica, Galatia, Colossae, Philippi and the other destinations of the New Testament epistles, clearly the answer is: through the **church**! Paul writes 'to the **church** of God in Corinth'; 'to the **churches** in Galatia'; 'to Nympha and the **church** in her house' (Colossians 4:15)'; 'to the **church** of the Thessalonians'. When he travelled back to Lystra, Iconium and Antioch after his church planting journey, he was concerned to strengthen the disciples by appointing elders in each **church** (Acts 14:23).

This suggests that we are right to make a powerful link between evangelism and church planting. For some groups in Britain today, evangelism is almost synonymous with church planting. This way of thinking is probably healthier than the one which sees evangelism as synonymous with an evangelistic crusade to fill up the existing churches' buildings, and make existing churches stronger. Certainly it is a good corrective to such thinking. In this 'evangelism equals church planting' model, the priority may be seen as a desire to make sure every community throughout the earth is covered by a church that is alive and preaching the good news of Jesus Christ. This would include putting a church in every housing estate so that members can speak to their neighbours about Christ, and bring his love in practical ways to the poor and the oppressed spiritually and physically. So another reason for church planting has to do with taking more ground for Jesus.

Not enough churches yet

Some may question whether we need new churches when there are so many half empty old church buildings. There are several answers to this. First, it may be that some of the old churches are resistant to change and to the gospel.

Leadership in some is weak, unbelieving and in some cases apostate. In these cases, new churches are definitely needed. Secondly, the old churches may not be unbelieving but so cautious as to move too slowly to win new people for Christ. In this case, not to plant churches is to leave thousands who would hear the gospel through the new church unable to hear it. Thirdly, a new church springing up may act as an incentive to older churches to reach out again with the gospel. To use a secular example: to open an antique shop next to another one is not necessarily bad marketing: the presence of two such shops in close proximity can bring in more custom!

Great care needs to be taken with ensuring good relationships between incoming church planters and established church leaders: ideally, a common strategy should be formed. Love and submission and mutual respect is certainly just as important as the success of the new church. This involves the incoming group taking the time and trouble to go and see other local leaders to talk through their plans. It is costly in terms of time and sometimes in terms of pride too. But it is vital: more of this later, in chapter 11.

But the main argument against the view that 'there are enough churches already' is that it depends what you mean by 'enough'. Dawn 2000 is a church planting movement which seeks to co-ordinate church planting efforts between the denominations and to set up networks and common strategies in every nation.[3] They have set a target of one viable, gospel preaching church for every thousand of the population. If this is a reasonable goal, we can thus greatly enlarge our vision. I live in a parish of 12,000 and a town of 30,000. This means a goal of thirty viable gospel preaching churches in our town and twelve in Cranham alone. At present, we have six, including Baptists and Roman Catholics: there is room for more! If we are to reach the tens of millions in our nation and the tens of thousands in our communities, how are we to do it if not through church planting? What other strategy is equal to the task? It is, quite simply, our future hope.

Church planting is not a strategy that is the property of any particular denomination or movement. Things are too urgent for that and the dynamic is too big for any group to claim ownership of it. But the movement is big enough and strategic enough for every single church grouping to get involved in it and to see again church planting as part of their *raison d'etre*.

By now many will be itching to get moving and so we turn immediately to the question: how can we get on with it?

3

Getting moving

In His will is our peace.

Dante

It may be that you are wanting to get on and be involved in something new for God. As one church planter has said: 'When Jesus comes back, I want to be *doing something* for God, even if it's only making mistakes.' Maybe you want to be cautious, knowing that to try and do a work of God by the flesh is to court disaster and possibly a nervous breakdown for good measure. This chapter mixes our personal story with principles from the book of Acts in the hope that it will help you to get on with it!

Looking through Acts at Paul's call to evangelise, which culminated in many churches being planted, we can see five stages through which he went. The passage which starts off all the activity is Acts 13 verses 2 and 3.

> While they were worshipping the Lord and fasting the Holy Spirit said, 'Set apart for me Barnabas and Saul [later named Paul] for the work to which I have called them.' So after they had fasted and prayed, they placed their hands on them and sent them off.

We see here for Paul first the **clear call** from God. Whether it came through prophecy, or perhaps through private prayer, we do not know. But Paul knew and the church knew. Next there was the **clear commission** from the church. Those who loved and supported Paul fasted and agreed with him and set him and Barnabas apart to do the work, giving away two of their most effective and valued leaders.

The next chapters reveal the **clear course of action** that the missionaries followed as they preached the gospel and established churches. This course of action involved an often violent struggle against unbelief and mistrust. They are expelled from the second city they visit (Acts 13:51), plotted against at the next (Acts 14:5), and nearly stoned to death at Lystra (Acts 14:19). This shows he is headed for a **clear collision** course with the opposition. But despite all this, Paul presses through by continuing the course of action. The fifth strand in their story is seen in the **clear conversions** to Christ that result. Because the ministry has been brought into being by God, the result is that it bears fruit, whether it is among the gentiles in Pisidian Antioch or the whole group of hearers in Lystra. The final consequence of all this activity is: new churches for which they appoint elders with prayer and fasting before returning to Antioch (Acts 14:23).

Clear call

The scope of our activity in Cranham is of course minute in comparison to these history making events, with fewer churches planted, fewer conversions and fewer persecutions! However, the principles for expansion have certainly obtained. First there was the clear call to the work which each team member felt. For myself, I remember going home after the AGM at which the idea to start the new church was first announced, wondering if it was to involve us in leadership. How were we to know if it was God's will? I once asked Alec Motyer, who was the wise and saintly principal of my theological college, how to hear the guidance of God, and he showed me some verses from Isaiah 50:4, 5 which he called a deep place of guidance in the Bible:

He wakens me morning by morning
  wakens my ear to listen like one being taught.
The Sovereign LORD has opened my ears,
  and I have not been rebellious . . .

Alec said that for him the daily instruction from the word of God in one's quiet time was the place where, over a period of weeks, we should receive guidance from God. This was just as important, if not more so, he said, than the flash of inspiration that comes out of the blue. And it was in this way that I clearly began to hear the call of God. Morning by morning in my regular reading, which at the time was in the Song of Songs, I heard the Lord calling me to a new stage in ministry.

  Arise . . . and come with me.
See! the winter is past;
  the rains are over and gone.
Flowers appear on the earth;
  The season of singing has come . . .
The fig-tree forms its early fruit . . .
Arise, come, my darling,
  my beautiful one, come with me.

These verses (from chapter 2) I received personally as an encouragement to 'Arise' and look for a new way of following Christ and preaching the gospel. I also received them on behalf of the new church that she dare to be intimate in worship of her Lord. Here was one type of call which was necessarily subjective. We tested it with another type which was the need: the new work needed a leader. We took advice from other friends, including our bishop, James Roxburgh, who all encouraged us to press ahead. All these came together and seemed to us a clear *call*, which we shared with the church.

We then set about gathering others for the work. All of

them were drawn together on the basis of a conviction similar to our own that God was calling them to something new. The call came in different ways. Some felt a leaping in their spirits at the moment when the announcement was made at the AGM, something which they knew was from God. Some came partly because of relationships with Annie and me. We had shared our lives and ministered with others in the faith sharing team and there was a sense that whatever we were in, we were in it together. Others came through visions. I remember once praying with a couple upon whom the Holy Spirit was powerfully moving. When we stopped, he told me that he saw Jesus leading him down the path away from St Luke's and out into the street. When he asked what this meant, he was convinced that he was to get up and go and join the church planting team. Others had no dramatic experience, but came because of the need. If you are part of a family and the washing up needs doing, you don't need a dramatic word from God to do it. Similarly, if you are in covenant relationship with others in a church, then when such a need arises it is quite reasonable to do it because it needs doing. So there are a multitude of different reasons for someone to join a church planting team. Having said this, each one must come by faith. That is to say, he or she must believe that it is God's will for him or her at that time.

A person should not join the team out of duty or obligation or persuasion from leadership, or solely because of the location of their home, unless they have faith that it is from God. We read that whatever does not proceed from faith is sin. Our experience is that it is possible to persuade unconvinced people to do something as drastic as this, but it is unwise and can lead to disaster. The most spiritual person, if not called to the group by God, can be a source of disunity. So it was that in our context 'the Holy Spirit said, "set apart for me" some sixteen dear brothers and sisters "for the work to which I have called them." ' We announced the formation of the team and began to meet weekly for prayer and worship and mutual ministry.

It is quite likely that with the call will come a 'special' understanding of the hallmarks of this new congregation. No two congregations are the same. God, the Lord of creation, sees to that. He is infinitely imaginative and careful in his creation. The church planting team will feel the touch of the potter moulding the clay into a new and unique vessel. In church growth terms it will be at this point that the leaders will be gaining the 'vision' for the work. This has almost become a technical term meaning philosophy of ministry or an understanding of, crudely, what they are there for. As the community church was formed, the vision was for 'intimacy'. It was not in this case a call to work in a particular area of the community, but rather it was a call to intimacy. Intimacy with God, with each other, and with the neighbourhood in which we lived, following the example of Jesus in John 1:14: 'The Word became flesh and lived for a while among us.'

The call was reflected in the name we eventually chose for the church: Cranham Community Church. We had from the outset a desire to cross barriers that had previously existed and to get involved in community groups. We considered buying a coffee bar and being a presence in the market place, but we realised this would not be a suitable place for Sunday worship, and our attempts to buy a suitable shop were consistently blocked. We then tried to rent a garage (long and thin and hence more the shape of a church!) but this fell through too. However we still had the calling from God. The call must come first, and with it comes the vision and the burden. All of us at this time began to understand what was meant by the scripture: 'Zeal for your house consumes me.' We began to experience something of the build up to labour pains.

Clear commission

At this point, in 1986, the mother church commissioned us to go and start the new church. In those days we still were unclear about how the work would develop and whether we would move towards independence or not. At the point of commissioning Paul, it may be that the elders in Antioch were not clear either. In many contexts, independence within a reasonable time scale may be the best option: but not necessarily. In the case of Ichthus Christian Fellowship in London, whose story we tell in chapter 4, to be an area church with different congregations dependent on one another has been preferred. On a smaller scale the same has obtained in many Anglican situations with great good effect. This vital dilemma is discussed later in chapter 11, along with the pros and cons of independence. Suffice it to say that at the point of commissioning it is a good idea to know which you are planting!

The fact of commissioning brings into focus the cost of church planting. What you are doing is giving away many of your best leaders. To begin with, members of the mother or core church may feel the pain of bereavement. In our context, as the community church started, there were rumblings and complaints and what we call '*gonguzmos*' (Greek and onomatopoeic for grumbling and moaning): 'All the life has gone out of us!' 'We've no direction.' 'I wish I'd gone with you.' 'We're not going anywhere!' Of course none of these remarks were justified.

It was true that some of the team who were sent were among those who were most experienced in the use of the gifts of the Spirit, but others soon emerged to take their place in the mother church. However, it did take some time for the mother church to readjust after this second labour and birth. This is the cost of church planting. Because of this cost, I would say one of the main requirements in church planting is that the leader of the mother church should be committed to giving away life. Sometimes this will mean giving away your strongest leaders; your most sacrificial givers; your steadiest workers. John Reeves has always taken almost more delight in doing this than anything else and I thank God for that. Many vicars or pastors want to hold on to their colleagues for dear life and cause them to be tied to two works rather than releasing them fully to one. I still remember on the morning the

Community Church opened, meeting John after the service. Beaming all over his face he related how he had told the mother congregation that he had woken up so happy . . . bursting with joy and excitement at the birth of a new baby . . . and they should be happy too! That is the spirit in which to get on with it.

In the end the mother church filled up again. This seems to be a law of church planting: give and it will be given to you. Now we plan to do it again, this time on the most difficult location, namely the council housing estate.

The commissioning is important for the owning of the project by the whole church. On this occasion we thought it so important that we invited the bishop to lay hands on the team as they were sent out and began to meet on Sunday mornings, initially in a large sitting room as we searched for suitable premises.

Commissioning services can be fairly dramatic occasions. I remember being present when a team of 100 was commissioned at the Anaheim Vineyard in California to plant a new church in the Los Angeles area. A prophecy was given which pictured a smartly dressed young man in a zip-up leather jacket. As the zip was undone, the man's guts and intestines fell out. The suggestion was that the people of the area were outwardly smart but inwardly seared with pain: bleeding inside. The people were to identify with this pain and share in God the Father's pain for his lost children. A wave of weeping and travail hit the hundred and men fell down and groaned, moved to intercede, as I understood it, by the Holy Spirit. When they had recovered a little and pain had given way to the peace of knowing that God was involved in the venture, John Wimber made a further suggestion. He called all others who felt a stirring to be involved in subsequent sending out of church planting teams to come forward. At least another hundred came and the work of equipping went on. It was a night to remember.

Although I have expected similar signs, our commissionings have on the whole been quiet affairs, at least until 1990. Then as we commissioned our team for what is at the time of writing known as the King's Arms church we experienced a pouring out of the gifts of the Spirit on those elders and leaders who were praying for the team: it seemed everyone had a word of instruction, a revelation, a tongue or an interpretation for the strengthening of the church. There was a fluency and an edification and upbuilding such as I have seldom seen. The result may sound surprising: it was laughter. Some in the team began to laugh until they cried.

Psalm 126 says: 'When the Lord brought back the captives to Zion, we were like men who dreamed. Our mouths were filled with laughter . . . those who sow in tears will reap with songs of joy.' To be aware that God is at work in a team and to be involved in his work can bring the profoundest joy. This can surprise us and overwhelm us so much that by far the most appropriate response is to laugh. Others in the team were being filled with the Spirit and others strengthened for the work of ministry.

When planting a new church, therefore, follow the Acts 13 pattern of the laying on of hands with prayer and fasting, and commission clearly the team for the work to which God has called them.

Clear course of action

Having been called and commissioned, then came the *course of action*, or the programme that followed the call. The programme is no good without the call but the call and vision have to be given shape by a pragmatic programme. It is unlikely a team will get all the details of its programme at the same time as the call to the work. They will have a common vision, but be unclear about the steps. This is biblical: Moses was clear about what he was to do, namely set the people free. But how he was to do it when face to face with Pharoah was far from certain. A more recent example is the call of David Wilkerson, author of *The Cross and the Switchblade* and founder of Teen Challenge. David tells about his night-time television viewing being interrupted by a prompting to pray; then of several trips to New

York all with no clear understanding that he was to set up a programme for those involved in drug abuse. The call of Jackie Pullinger into a similar programme was equally unspecific to start with. After checking it out with her church leader, she took a boat to Hong Kong! The highly organised St Stephen's Society programme which she now leads was at that time a closed book to her! The church planting team must be willing to seek God and support its leader as he tries to work out the programme as he proceeds: this calls for patience!

But having been called and commissioned, we should expect the programme to take shape. This may be helped by finding out more about your community. Who lives there? What are the felt needs, aspirations, hopes, fears? A survey is a very helpful way to begin to research the areas intelligently. We reproduce in the appendix one that our new church planting team are currently using.

Following this, it may be that a plan of action emerges. In the case of our community church we were aware of the apparent separation or rift between community groups and church. Our plan formed to become intimately involved in our community, and where better to start than *via* a group like our community association? I remember my first visit to the home of the chairman of this group. Much to my surprise he was just at the point of actively seeking more support, and so a relationship began between church and community association which has developed and grown . . . as has, incidentally, the friendship between their respective leaders.

Clear collision with the opposition

This was the plan: intimate involvement in our community. But almost as soon as our church team was formed, with the desire of being a marvellous example of love in action, we found we could not get on together, let alone with the world! The new church should not be dismayed at trouble within or without in the early stages: it may well come as a result of being on a collision course with the forces of evil who, putting it bluntly, do not want the new church to survive!

In this period of the first twelve months of the life of the new church we experienced doubt, uncertainty and spiritual attack. It says in Revelation 12:4, 'The dragon stood in front of the woman who was about to give birth, so that he might devour her child the moment it was born.' Applying this to the body of Christ in Cranham, the very week that I finalised the membership of the team and announced it, one couple in the team had a violent row with others and left the new work and also the church. We lost a man whom I had seen come to Christ, who was very gifted in personal evangelism, whom I saw as vital to the work and as a personal friend. With hindsight, I know I should have seen the warning signals in the man himself, which I missed through inexperience, but the result was that a cloud of depression, a sense of failure, settled over me, and also over the whole team. So the struggle began for unity.

There was also a struggle for premises: we were meeting in a home which limited growth and every door we tried to open remained tightly shut. We tried shops, a garage, a school, a social centre, pubs – and all were unavailable. There was a struggle for conversions: one or two people professed to give their lives to Christ but soon fell away. We entered a barren period. Put all these together and there was a struggle for faith. Were we on the right track at all? I remember ringing Campbell McAlpine, to whom I turn at times of crisis. The conversation would go something like this. 'How's the new church going?' 'Slowly.' 'Well, that's how you grow big trees.' So we pressed through with the course of action.

At such a time, it is good to remember that if the new church is to take territory for Jesus there may well be spiritual forces with whom you are on collision course. The effects may not seem to have anything to do with the work, but if disunity and depression occur it's quite likely that there is an unseen cause. David Watson used to say: 'Much of the church's warfare today is fought by blindfolded soldiers who cannot see the forces ranged against them, who are buffeted by invisible opponents and respond by striking one another.'

Opinions differ as to how such 'invisible opponents' operate, and we will return to this vital subject in chapter 13. But in the collision course, the church has some mighty weapons. Prayer is the first. If a church finds itself divided but comes together in spite of this to pray and fast and repent and seek God for a renewal of love, then unity and power can be restored from within and a breakthrough occur. Praise is another great weapon to 'silence the foe and the avenger' (Psalm 8). When these weapons are taken out on to the streets, it can lead to a change in the spiritual climate, of which more later.

Perhaps, above all, the way to pull down these strongholds is by telling people about Jesus. Paul says 'the weapons we fight with . . . have divine power to demolish strongholds. We demolish arguments and every pretension that sets itself up against the knowledge of God' (2 Corinthians 10:4–5). It is quite likely that preaching and debating about Jesus is what Paul had in mind. Oh that every member of the new church would be filled with boldness: that when in collision with opposition they would respond – not by hitting each other – but by clearly telling their neighbours and community about Jesus! May they go on and on telling about him as they pursue their course of action.

Continuing the course of action

One day at 6.00 am we walked up to a disused school in our community and stood outside praying. I discovered it was to become a community centre – but not for eighteen months. We applied to hire it but were told it was not available until refurbished and handed over to the community association. We prayed through and renewed our application in person to the councillor concerned.

To cut a long story short, the church was granted special provision to use the building twelve months before it

You know you're in church planting when . . .
anything that breathes is counted in Sunday attendance.

became generally available; I was elected to the executive and later became a trustee of the community centre. We were involved in choosing furniture and carpeting for the centre at a cost of thousands of pounds, although we didn't pay for it. I, and then later my secretary, were given offices in this secular building, as the committee agreed this would help meet the pastoral needs of the community. One of our church members became the paid administrator for the centre in which now, two years after we used it first and one year after it opened to the public, there are dance classes; keep fit; carpet bowls; drama; OAP's club; card club; ballroom dancing; judo etc. It has become a hive of activity. Instead of starting our own clubs and groups, I have encouraged our members to be as salt in many of the different activities of the centre. When we began, we therefore had six members helping lead the open youth club; one who headed up and organised a coffee bar which aims to be open whenever the centre is open; others who were involved in the drama; keep fit; OAP's and other groups. As regards the growth of the church, about a year after beginning to meet, slowly but surely we began to grow.

Clear conversions

First it was lost Christians who came. They had no church affiliation: some were hurt, others were strong, but they all found they could commit themselves heart and soul to what we were doing. And then, as numbers increased and it became less difficult for non-Christians to come, we saw several wonderful conversions. Here, in their own brief words, are the stories of just three of them.

First, Carol Dare's story as it appeared in our church magazine:

> When the Children's Christian Crusade came to St Luke's last year, I took my son James along. I noticed how happy people were, which was something I hadn't known for a long time.
>
> Then Ron and I started taking James to Sunday School at the Community Church. I went along to some services and again I saw how happy people were. I wanted to go more often but didn't feel confident enough to do so. I met Charlie, and he asked me to come along to the Mothering Day Service. I went and had a lovely time. During that week I felt the Lord speak to me and I knew that this is what I'd been looking for all my life and I decided to follow Jesus.
>
> I still have dark days, but now I have *hope* and I know that the Lord will keep me safe.
>
> Psalm 34:4 sums up how I feel about the Lord: 'I sought the LORD, and he answered me; he delivered me from all my fears.'

Now Paul Shooter, a deputy head teacher, gives his story:

My wife first introduced me to Cranham Community Church about a year ago. She had been rededicated at St Luke's a year previous to that. At first I found the Community Church very strange (all that arm waving, holding hands up, etc.). But one thing I was impressed with was the friendliness of everybody and the obvious joy that everybody felt. Unfortunately for a while my attendance at church was very patchy and I wouldn't think about the church or God for weeks on end. My heart was hardened to the Word of God. After a while my wife suggested that we to go Spring Harvest at Minehead (a week of celebration and worship etc. with 10,000 Christians). Whilst waiting to go to Spring Harvest my visits to church became more regular and I began to realise the truth of God's Word. The week at Minehead proved very enjoyable and away from work I found time to read some very interesting books. On returning from Spring Harvest (and back to work) I found that I was constantly thinking about God, Jesus, being a Christian. I realised the truth of all I had heard and read and decided to give my heart to Jesus and ask God to forgive me my sins on Wednesday, 13th April in the car on the way home from work. It was the best decision I have ever made in my life.

Finally, Terry Steventon, a fifty-five year old electrical engineer, writes:

Jeane, Ann and Jenny attended Cranham Community Church a year ago but I was not interested: too busy doing something or other. Then, last summer, Claudia our Italian friend stayed with us and Jeane asked if she would like to come to the Community Church. She said she would! So I had to come as well or be the perfect Male Chauvinist Pig. Claudia was very impressed by the friendly reception she received. She was not the only one to be impressed. Little did I know that I was hooked. I actually began to look forward to coming here, and my family couldn't believe it! Then things took off from there. I joined the Welcome Group and one evening, not long ago, we had been discussing commitment and how we felt about it. Everyone said what they thought and I said I had always believed in God and Jesus Christ due to my upbringing, personal feelings and experiences but I found commitment difficult. Then Lydia, who was part of the group, had a go at me and said you had to put your whole being into Christ's hands and trust him to do the rest. It struck me that Jenny, my daughter, had said similar words to me years ago, and I had ignored them. I realised I could no longer pussyfoot around! Then at the end of the meeting the leader of the group asked me to stay behind. He asked if I was ready to commit myself to the Lord. I said yes and said the prayer of repentance and commitment which he prayed with me. At the end, no voices, no blinding light, just a feeling of contentment and peace. One thing I realised about my renewal of my faith is that I had nothing to do with it!

At the time of writing, the church has grown from sixteen adults two years ago to a regular attendance of over 100. Where there was one mid-week housegroup there are now six and we have a common goal of raising this number to ten such groups by the end of the year.

To get on with it, therefore, we need first to seek God and hear his *call*. When this has been tested and discussed and agreed, we will do well clearly to *commission* a team for the work. Then follows the pushing through of the *course of action* despite buffetings and any opposition. Finally, the fruit of the work will be seen as ordinary people *find Christ* through this new local expression of his love.

4

The state of the art
I: Some current initiatives in church planting

Christ came to establish a new society on earth. It was not enough for him to call individual sinners to God. He promised that He would build his church. It would be the most powerful force on earth.

David Watson

The 1980s saw a new wave of activity in Britain. Many groups and denominations began to plant new churches in schools, disused church buildings and halls and pubs up and down the country. Space allows us only to look at some of the most significant of these developments here.

Spurgeon's, Oasis and the Baptists
A major initiative was the setting up of a degree course in Church Planting and Evangelism at Spurgeon's College. This was announced in the Spring 1989 *Spurgeon's Record*: 'A degree level course in evangelism, the first in the country, is to be launched at Spurgeon's College next autumn.' So ran the first paragraph introducing the venture. 'We are now going back to our roots,' said Principal Paul

Beasley-Murray. 'In his day our founder Charles Spurgeon and his men planted about 160 churches. For many years we in Britain thought of church growth as building bigger buildings for more people. Now we see that it means planting new churches – this is an exciting project for the future.'

The course is a joint project of Spurgeon's College and the Oasis Trust and in effect it provides a choice for candidates for the Baptist ministry. The choice is between training for the pastoral ministry or training for the church planting and evangelistic ministry. Students wanting to take the new course live out of college, serving in local areas, learning by doing – they work in housing estates or inner city areas under the direction of the tutor and they go to Spurgeon's two days a week for lectures, seminars and tutorials. Time will tell how this course can best be adapted to serve Christ at the end of the twentieth century. But it certainly represents a bold and timely initiative on the part of those involved in theological education. It is precisely such initiatives from denominations that are needed if the decline in church membership is to be halted. The course opened in 1989 with six students and after these small beginnings an annual application of ten, building to a course total of forty, is expected.

Between 1980 and 1985 a remarkable thing happened to the Baptist denomination. Decline turned to growth. For a major British denomination this was unheard of. It reflects the clarifying of vision that has occurred among Baptists and it reflects a return to its evangelical roots. The selection of men of proven evangelistic and church growth ability such as David Coffey as Evangelism Secretary at Baptist House and Douglas MacBain as General Superintendent of the Metropolitan Area (the Baptists' 'Bishop of London') was greeted with shouts of joy in the present writer's hearing. That these men, and others, have been chosen reflects a growing desire in the local churches for direction. And these men are now giving it! So it is that for Douglas MacBain it is a clearly defined aim to consider setting targets for numbers of churches to be planted in the coming decade and to work to facilitate this. Similarly in the north of England men like Harry Weatherley, until recently the Baptist Union's Yorkshire Association's Missioner, see as one of their goals the planting of churches before the end of the millennium. Geoffrey Reynolds, Southern Area Superintendent, has worked to develop an associational strategy for planting new churches, helping colleagues to gain an overall view of areas of growth and of need in the south. In October 1990 a network of Baptist Church planters was officially formed gathering around a hundred ministers and aiming to hold a first residential conference in 1991.

The House Churches

When church statistics paint a picture of general decline, a movement which grows at the rate of two congregations each week is a striking feature. Rod Borcham, editor of *Team Spirit* magazine gives this description of their beginnings. 'In the late 'sixties those who now lead this movement wanted to get away from a Christianity that was centred around buildings and meetings and give time to developing relationships. Thus were the House Churches born. The mould was broken . . . their meetings began literally in homes but quickly outgrew front rooms so moved to larger venues. However big they grew, the name "House Church" seemed to stick.'

Although insignificant in overall size (120,000 members in 1990 as opposed to the Church of England's 1,824,000: MARC Europe figures from the *UK Christian Handbook 1989/90*), the chart shows their growth. Through events like Spring Harvest their influence is enormous on church life across the denominations. It is certainly out of proportion to their actual size, but is in my view a healthy thing. It shows that they have got something which the traditional denominations badly need to relearn.

From their early emphasis on relationship as opposed to religion, and an initial growth from Christians transferring from denominational churches, it is fair to say that mission

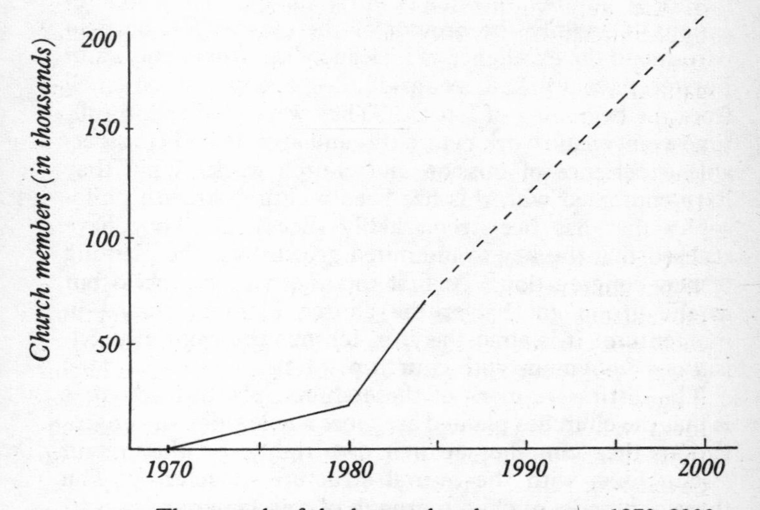

The growth of the house church movement 1970–2000. (Dotted lines link estimated figures.)

and church planting now feature high on the whole movement's agenda as never before. At their 1988 conference, four keynote sessions were given over to what was entitled 'Church Planting – Our Future Hope', which just about sums it up.

Ichthus

Broadly speaking Ichthus is part of the House Church movement. They have been a major force in church planting in south-east London in the 1980s. The church began in 1974 under the leadership of Roger Forster and grew to a congregation of 250 by 1980, since which time it experienced a rapid growth to a 1985 membership of over 1000 people meeting in fifteen different congregations and by 1990 this growth reached over 1700 adult members, not including children, meeting in thirty-three different congregations. Certainly the growth of the church has been in part due to the excellence of its leadership. Roger and Faith Forster have worked alongside Roger and Sue Mitchell from the beginning of Ichthus. They were involved in full-time evangelistic work before this and already had considerable experience of mission and church work. What they have combined with this has been a church growth philosophy that has been remarkably successful. They have realised that the key to unlimited growth was the planting of new congregations. At first this was a slow process but as the group got bigger the church planting gained in momentum. It is almost as if in Ichthus the word evangelism is synonymous with church planting.

The distinctive mark of these church planting activities is that the churches planted are more a federation of congregations than churches in their own right, and they retain strong links with the overall structure of Ichthus. The threefold model of church growth of cell, congregation and celebration works at Ichthus to great effect. The first tier of life is the cell, or housegroup of eight to twenty people, and these are constantly multiplied. The second tier of life is the congregation, and as this grows to around 100 to 200 people it will want to combine with other congregations from Ichthus to plant a new congregation in a new area. The third tier of life is the celebration, to which all the congregations will go. In this way in any given week a member of Ichthus Christian Fellowship will find himself attending a cell on Wednesday night, his own local congregation on Sunday morning and probably the Sunday celebration, for all the congregations of Ichthus, on Sunday night. In 1988 the celebration meeting was numbering around 2000 people and facilities at the school at which the meeting was taking place were being stretched. Evidently there was a need to split into two large gatherings and this occurred, and eventually a further split into three.

What is appealing about the structure at Ichthus is the logic with which it is all applied: each Christian can be involved in a small group that can be healthy, supportive and can help the Christian to be involved in caring for the people immediately around where he lives. And Christians can be involved in the local congregation for mutual ministry and encouragement and evangelism on a slightly larger scale. Children can be involved, at the local congregation level, in a church where they are valued, and the Sunday morning service will have a family feel and be fairly low key and be an easy place for non-Christians to go. Evangelism will take place through these services. The celebration enables each Christian to be involved with a wider movement with all the encouragement and growth in vision and understanding of less parochial concerns that that brings.

Ichthus has grown through a combination of traditional evangelistic methods and of rediscovery of powerful ministry in the Holy Spirit. But the church also has a strong emphasis on social action and members will involve themselves in local concerns and politics as necessary. They will also be concerned to engage in spiritual warfare. When they want to plant a new congregation they will go into the area and march with musicians and singers around the area declaring the lordship and rule of Jesus. This has a threefold effect; it is to fight a spiritual battle and to proclaim the authority of Jesus in a new area. But it also raises the visibility of the Christians, and as people enquire what's going on they can be informed that a new congregation will soon be started.

One of the keys to Ichthus' growth has been the strong emphasis from the beginning on training. It may be that the Spurgeon's course has grown out of what Ichthus have pioneered. From the beginning they took on 'trainees' in evangelism and church planting, first one at a time and then in small groups and now they run a carefully organised evangelistic training programme called Network. No doubt it is because of the vision to train in this way that Ichthus has been able to grow in the way that it has done. When I asked Roger Forster whether they had ever started a new congregation without a full-time worker he replied that it was not that they were in principle against it, but in practice they had not done so. One of the principal factors causing the growth in church planting activity to dry up in other situations is the lack of full-time leaders to take on the work. Any church which wishes consistently to plant new congregations must, it seems, take seriously the need to train new leaders who can make themselves fully available to this work. In other situations this doctrine will be considered an anathema, for example in the Assemblies of God it is fairly common for a church planter to have secular employment. But, in my experience, if this is the case although it is possible to plant a new church it will not happen nearly as quickly as it will do if someone can make themselves available full-time.

The lessons to be learned from Ichthus are manifold: they have a very clear philosophy of ministry involving a threefold emphasis on mission, fellowship and training. There is a clear understanding among the members of the goals and emphases of the congregation, and there is a clear understanding of church growth methods among the leaders. This has made it possible to set goals for growth, under the guidance of the Holy Spirit, and to hit them.

Cobham's Pioneer Team

Another model for church planting is provided by the church which began in the 1970s in Cobham, led by the irrepressible Gerald Coates. Gerald has been known to coin such memorable one-liners as the following: 'If the joy of the Lord is our strength, it's little wonder that the church in Britain has been so weak and ineffective'; 'There's no virtue in being ten or twenty years behind the times'; 'Most Christians are nicer than God himself'; 'It is the unshared areas of our lives where Jesus is not Lord'; 'One of the reasons the church in Britain has failed to grow is quite simply because it is full of people who are extremely rude'; 'Putting the life of God into institutional Christianity is rather like putting the life of a human being into a kangaroo . . .' 'You are only a leader if someone's following you' (*Gerald Quotes*).

From the '70s to the '80s the handful which initially was Cobham Christian Fellowship grew to number 250, and since the mid-1980s the group has been committed to church planting. This reflects the general evolution of the new churches whose emphasis has shifted away from being a community, enjoying being a family and enjoying God. The current priority is the planting of churches and evangelising whole communities, without – it is to be hoped – forgetting lessons learned about community.

The Cobham model is significant to church planters in that some of those involved in leadership believe they have already gone through certain different models for church planting before reaching their present most favoured version. The first plant was in Farnham, some twenty miles from Cobham, in the mid-'80s. One leader took between fifteen and twenty people, hired a hall, broke the link with the Cobham Fellowship and began to establish a church which has grown to some sixty members. In 1987 a team of twenty went to Molsey and now number eighty or ninety. In 1988 a larger team moved to Tooting, at the invitation of the Shaftesbury Society, and in eighteen months grew to a group of 150 attending worship, of whom 70% are new converts. Here they have found that one convert will lead his or her family to Christ. Growth has been faster by means of these 'bridges of God', to use Donald McGavran's phrase. As Christians have found, 'One shall tell another and he shall tell his friends. Husband, wife and children shall come following on . . .' (Graham Kendrick). In 1989/90 a further group moved to Leatherhead and another to Wandsworth as the church planting began to gain momentum. At the same time, the Cobham Fellowship itself formed five smaller congregations from the one large group, only meeting twice a month as one church. They now have a structure for faster growth in Cobham itself.

Steve Clifford, one of the Cobham leaders with whom some of these teams consult regularly, identifies various desirable features which facilitate growth, believing that in Tooting many of these came together whereas in the earlier attempts, one or more of these elements was missing. The first is the presence of a 'breakthrough person'. This is a leader who has evangelistic gifts, is essentially outward looking, as well as having the ability to lead and relate well to a team. Again and again we find this the single most important factor in church planting. Reflecting on this, one issue for all churches desiring to grow is whether they are prepared to bring through such people into leadership. This is in some ways a departure for many house churches which have been strongly pastoral in emphasis.

The second factor relates to the first and concerns the make up of the team. If the real interest of all team members is pastoral and relational, they won't do as well as the group which contains a variety of gifts. It is unhelpful to send a team of administrators when there is nothing to administer! What is needed are some prophets, some evangelists, some pastors and teachers (Ephesians 4: 11–12), some whose gift is to serve, some to contribute to the needs of others, some to encourage, some to lead (but not all), some to show mercy cheerfully (Romans 12: 6–8). In addition, the team will do well if the Holy Spirit is manifested through wisdom, knowledge, faith, healing, miracles, discernment of spirits, prophecy, tongues and interpretation (1 Corinthians 12: 8–12).

In Tooting, one element that has been particularly important has been the experience of the miraculous. Through a simple presentation in some summer tent healing meetings, people saw God at work in changing lives physically and spiritually, and the breakthrough sought in evangelism was experienced through this vital means. Another further piece in the puzzle was the presence of a Training In Evangelism team full-time with the new church for the first year of its life. Again, as with Ichthus, we see that the training of leaders is written into the church planting strategy, and it is clear that for churches to grow they need to invest in more leaders. Cobham Fellowship have for several years run two week, one month or one year training for future leaders. A final ingredient to throw into the church planting pot was a clearer link kept with the Cobham Fellowship or at least the Pioneer Leadership Team. Where this was retained, growth occurred more effectively.

Summing all this up, the Pioneer Church Planting Cookbook Recipe might look something like this:

1. take one key leader, a 'breakthrough person';
2. target an area in prayer and research;
3. take fifteen to twenty-five Christians of different gifts and abilities, especially including evangelists and healers;
4. move to the area in question;
5. evangelise by friendship and by high profile healing meetings;
6. add a small full-time short term training team;
7. retain close ties with home base: keep in contact;
8. stir in prayer;
9. wait expectantly for explosion in the oven.

As a postscript, the question may immediately be posed: what if we haven't got all these ingredients and can't get hold of them? The answer is that you can still proceed. You may find that growth is slower, or you may find that God provides as you step out in faith. The above 'recipe' describes one group's insights so far, coming out of less than a decade of such activity. Others can and do work in a different way. Weakness can be a bonus provided it leads us to depend on God himself. Some teams will need to be encouraged by the Lord's word to the fearful Gideon who had been called to fight the Midianites. He was told this: 'Go in the strength you have . . . Am I not sending you?' (Judges 6: 14).

Pentecostal planning

Another potentially radical strand in the story of church planting comes from a group of men leading the north-west England area of the Elim Pentecostal Church. David Tinnion and Phil Weaver have produced a video called *Breakthrough 2000* outlining their scheme. Their vision is simple: to plant 100 new churches in their area by the end of the decade, using a base of around sixty-six already functioning Elim churches in the north-west. Once the scheme was adopted, comments were sought from certain nationally respected leaders.

Roy Pointer: 'I have been asking for over ten years that there needs to be some bold plans, mission strategy, developed within the denominations and I have not been aware of any until now. This ("Breakthrough 2000") is the kind of project that needs to be on every denomination's agenda. I think "Breakthrough 2000" will be a model for many other districts and provinces and maybe other denominations too.'

Clive Calver notes four things in its favour: 'One – it sets goals and avoids the waffle of "we are seeking God for spiritual growth". There will be egg on people's faces if the 100 is not reached. I would rather die in a glorious cause than to succeed because I never set anything to go for. Two – it has good spiritual leadership. Three – it is not afraid of dreaming; of going into new methods, new concepts, new ways of reaching people. Church planting is, I sense, so much at the heart of God for this country at this moment. Four – the concentration in using the whole people of God in evangelism and commitment.'

Ian Coffey of the Evangelical Alliance: 'I just sense this to be a confirmation of what God is saying to the church. It may have an Elim label on it, but I think "Breakthrough 2000" is a vision from God that deserves wider exposure. "Breakthrough 2000" warmed my heart because I think: here is vision, here is faith, and here are people who are setting a target and they are wanting to move towards it.'

I agree that this scheme is significant not only because of what may be achieved for good in the north-west, but because it can act as a model for planning for other areas and for other denominations.

It is interesting also that this scheme goes back to the roots of the Elim movement. After a large crusade the Jeffreys would appoint a leader and give him the task of planting a new church with the fruits of the crusade. The Jeffreys in fact would not have understood an Elim movement that was not planting churches. Just as the new Spurgeon's/Oasis venture goes back to Baptist roots, so do the organisers of 'Breakthrough 2000' believe they are going back to roots. In this sense, both are truly radical signs of life!

Youth With A Mission

Most missionary societies have been planting churches as part of their primary activity since the start of the so called 'missionary movement' in the last century. But it is interesting that in the 1980s even some of those that didn't plant churches began to move in the direction of doing so. One of the largest such groups is Youth With A Mission, or YWAM. In 1980 a conference was held in Thailand for the organisation's leaders. They concluded that God was calling them to plant churches. Before this YWAM had seen themselves solely as a youth evangelistic organisation that was an outreach arm of existing churches.

In 1990 Floyd McClung published a paper outlining 'Ten reasons why Youth With A Mission plants churches'[1]. The reasons given are as follows. First, it is the biblical pattern. Second, planting churches lays a foundation for discipling whole nations. Third, church planting is how unreached cities, nations and peoples will be reached with the gospel. Fourth, church planting reaches all levels of society because the gospel is spread through family and relationship networks. Fifth, churches are planted because this preserves the fruit of YWAM's evangelism. Sixth, YWAM plants churches because they are a vital place of nurture for multi-generational groups of believers. Seventh, believers in newly planted churches have the responsibility to grow in evangelistic and missionary maturity. Eighth, they plant churches because 'God wants YWAM missionaries to build into local congregations the spiritual foundations' he has given tham as a mission. Ninth, they feel they should be a channel by which church planters may move to the countries where they are needed. Tenth, they plant churches to train church planters.

This is a signifcant change for the fastest growing mission organisation in Britain. YWAM's church planting activity will be more evident among unevangelised peoples, but will also affect Britain and Europe in the 1990s. They are at pains to insist that they are not called to be a denomination. When church planting where churches already exist, the new churches are instructed to become part of existing networks or denominations. The implication is that, depending on the preference of the church planter, YWAM may plant Baptist, Anglican, house church or another type of church, but not YWAM churches!

YWAM do not want to discontinue their current policy of encouraging in every way current initiatives for church planting and feeding people in to help such work. But at the same time, they are to start planting new churches. Time will tell how well these twin goals work together. But we will hear more of this in years to come and it is yet another sign that church planting is on God's agenda at this time for Britain, for Europe, and for every nation.

The Vineyard

Another international initiative is the planting of Vineyard churches in England, which began in 1987 when John and Eleanor Mumford arrived back from California. John Mumford had been a curate in the Church of England with a significant ministry and had gone for a year's sabbatical to California. During this time it had become clear to him that, to use his phrase, 'the Holy Spirit had separated' him to the Vineyard movement which is led by John Wimber. The movement had had an enormous impact on Christian leaders throughout England in the previous years – few churches have not benefitted from the faith and New Testament life of the movement. This is not the place to analyse the whys and wherefores of John's call from one denomination into another movement. There are obviously personal and spiritual reasons that motivated such a call. But from a pragmatic point of view one of the main motives would have been the desire to plant churches which were capable of reproducing themselves. Within the Anglican denomination the major frustration for the church planter is the parochial system. This effectively prevents a church naturally reproducing and having babies. If a church has grown to a membership of 300 and wishes to send one of its leaders and several of its members to start a new and similar flourishing work in a neighbouring area it may meet with problems. An application to the bishop for permission may be met with either incomprehension or with the calm statement that there is already a church in the neighbouring parish. We will speak more of this in a later chapter.

John and Eleanor arrived back in London in June 1987 and John took a secular job. By September 1987 they had one small housegroup. Their aim was to start from the bottom up and to grow a church that would be able in the end to plant other churches. At this time there were nine in the housegroup and according to John they were a motley bunch. By December of the same year they had two similar groups and by March 1988, three and at this stage they began to meet all together monthly for a celebration. By September 1988 there were six such groups meeting fortnightly with a membership of about a dozen each. There were still no Sunday meetings. John would say that too many groups begin to meet on Sundays too soon. This is standard Vineyard philosophy. In these early days there were various mottos: the first was to keep their eye off numbers, the second was to have fun, the third was not to recruit anyone and the fourth was not to defend themselves. As the church began to take shape the fivefold Vineyard philosophy of ministry began to be applied and still forms the church's reason for being. These five priorities are:

1. worship
2. teaching
3. ministry
4. training
5. sending.

By 1989 the church was meeting in fortnightly celebrations in Raynes Park High School and at the time of writing the church has grown to a membership of 300.

One might ask how the church has grown if it is not out to recruit members from other denominations. Has the church grown through traditional evangelistic methods of knocking on doors, evangelising, leafleting streets and campaigning in the open air? The answer is none of these things have been undertaken as strategies for the church. In fact, John Mumford's view would be that just as the church needed a new model for healing (and it was in some degree provided when John Wimber and his team came to train church leaders from many different denominations and streams in England), so a new model is needed for evangelistic ministry. The average Briton finds someone knocking at his door extremely embarrassing and someone performing on the streets and handing out tracts equally uncomfortable. This leads John Mumford to seek for a new model in evangelism. The way that the church has grown in the meantime is simply through word of mouth. Those who have come into a home meeting or into the public celebrations have met God in an unmistakable way. It may be that they have been healed; it may be that they have known the manifest presence of God as the church has drawn near to him in worship. It may be that they have been without God and alone and lost in the world and that through the preaching of the word they have become Christians. In these and other ways the church has grown.

Other leaders have gone over to the Anaheim Vineyard for training. Among them are Rick and Lulu Williams, and Chris and Flis Lane. Both Rick and Chris were also ministers in the Church of England before their flight to California! They are now back in this country in the process of establishing new Vineyard churches. This has not been without considerable sacrifice and testing of faith. Whatever 'security' there may be in the working for the Church of England has been lost. Each has on return to this country gone back into secular employment to finance the starting of the new church. Each has known the struggle and patient endurance of beginning such a work. The signs are that God is blessing these initiatives with his presence and his Spirit and it is unlikely that the growth of the Vineyard in Britain will stop there.

The church planting initiatives examined in this chapter provide much inspiration. But are these models adequate for the Church of England? We move on to examine this crucial question.

5

The state of the art

II: One a month

It hath been the wisdom of the church of England, ever since the first compiling of her Publick Liturgy, to keep the mean between two extremes, of too much stiffness in refusing, and of too much easiness in admitting any variation from it . . .

Preface to the 1662 Book of Common Prayer

A significant development in church planting in the 1980s was within the Church of England, although in this case the growth was not without frustrations. In June 1987 a first day conference on church planting was held at Holy Trinity Brompton; more were held in 1988 and 1989 with a further conference held at St Andrew's, Chorleywood in 1989. In the north of England similar days were held. These reflected a growing interest in church growth and a desire to find a way to grow the church which did not just find its expression in building bigger buildings. In 1989 the *Church of England Newspaper* had a banner headline informing its readership that 'One New Church a Month' was being planted. In the context of declining overall membership (a 29% drop in the twenty years to 1990) and a reduction in the number of ministers (down 16% in the twenty years to 1990) this was an encouraging sign which the denomination would do well to learn from. (Figures are from the *UK Christian Handbook 1989/90.*) It shows that there are areas in the life of the Church of England where confidence is high.

Church planting within the parish

Broadly speaking, the church planting activity in the Church of England should be divided into two kinds. The first type is within the parish and is significant but limited; the second is across parish boundaries and is extremely difficult! Within the parish, on countless occasions, churches have identified areas which are relatively unevangelised and taken several members and planted them out there. Typically, such a team is led by a curate who may gain an extension to his contract and stay for two to three years to establish the work.

One such example occurred in Nailsea, near Bristol. There the curate, John Carter, had the joy of establishing a new work in the local pub. In this case the main stumbling block was seen as staffing for the new venture as the church was already fully stretched. Then the opportunity of having an unexpected extra curate was presented to them by George Carey, then Bishop of Bath and Wells, in late July and a new leader moved with his family into the Carters' house at the end of September. Meanwhile the diocese not only supplied an extra man but very quickly went about finding a house on the Trendlewood estate for the Carter family to move into (at a cost of £125,000) – so very generous and rapid support from the diocese was a key factor. From October '88 when he moved in, John began to build a team together – nine married couples (most of whom held responsibilities in the main church) were released to concentrate on Trendlewood.

As the work began, one of those beautiful coincidences organised by God took place: the only public building on the Trendlewood estate (indeed the only building not a house) was the Old Farmhouse pub. It so happened that when John approached the manager and his wife they had only just been moved to the pub with the brief to try and improve relations between the pub and the local community. It seemed to be a green light to both sides, the brewery's only concern being that they weren't Jehovah's Witnesses or Christian Scientists! The team began experimenting there in December '88 and by the end of January it was felt right to go for a public launch on Palm Sunday '89 with attendant door to door visiting with invitations, and publicity to the press and media. The article below from *The Daily Telegraph* is just one example of press coverage received.

Church finds room at the inn

Beer mats will give way to hymnals, and glasses to enlightenment as Britain's first 'pub church' holds its Easter Day service, two hours before opening time at the Old Farmhouse public house in Nailsea, near Bristol.

Holy Trinity Trendlewood, founded a week ago, is a church without walls, meeting at parishioners' homes on weekday evenings, and in the dining lounge of the Old Farmhouse on Sundays.

The pub is the only public building serving the Trendlewood estate and its 3,000 residents. The nearest church was several miles away until the curate, the Revd John Carter, approached the landlords of the Old Farmhouse, Mr Kevin Thomas and his wife, Shirley.

'People thought it was an early April Fool's joke at first,' he said last week. 'But they are all behind it. The manager and staff of the pub get on with things in the background, behind screens, during the service. They say they like the sound of singing, which gives them a bit of a boost at the beginning of the day.'

The Bishop of Bath and Wells, the Rt Revd George Carey, blessed Holy Trinity Trendlewood as 'an exciting initiative which I very much hope we will see repeated in other places.'

Mr Carter said nothing in the Bible prohibited worship in a pub. 'Jesus was, of course, born in an inn, though admittedly in an outbuilding because there was no room inside. And he did turn water into wine.'

The wine for today's Communion was not from the Old Farmhouse bar. 'We provide our own special variety,' said Mr Carter. 'I don't know whether we will have to pay corkage.'

It is interesting to note differing timescales in church planting activity. In this case, the idea for a new church was in the leader's mind for over a year before conception. This took place with the arrival of replacement staff (setting John free to lead the work), the purchase of accommodation and then the formation of the team in the autumn of 1988. By December the team were meeting in the pub, ready for the birthday in April.

From a committed team of nine couples, less than a year later they have the encouragement of now seeing a hundred regularly worshipping together each week.

Bob Hopkins, Anglican church planting co-ordinator, and George Lings, database organiser, have identified various motivations for starting new congregations of this kind. These can include: inadequate parish penetration; growth philosophy, new housing opportunity, physical restrictions at the mother church and in some cases the bishop's initiative, as the chart on page 62 shows. (The data describes the 88 'new' Anglican churches planted between 1967 and 1988 in the UK.)

Our own experience was that our first and third church sprang from awareness of inadequate parish penetration. Our second and fourth sprang from physical restrictions at the mother church and from church growth philosophy.

Whatever the motivation, church planting can be recognised as a powerful means for enabling our churches to grow. Even if churches planted start very small, they can still grow much faster than larger ones. Statistics for the diocese of Sheffield covering the period '82 to '88 show – as Table 1 demonstrates[1] – that when it comes to attendance growth, small is beautiful. The attendance growth can be

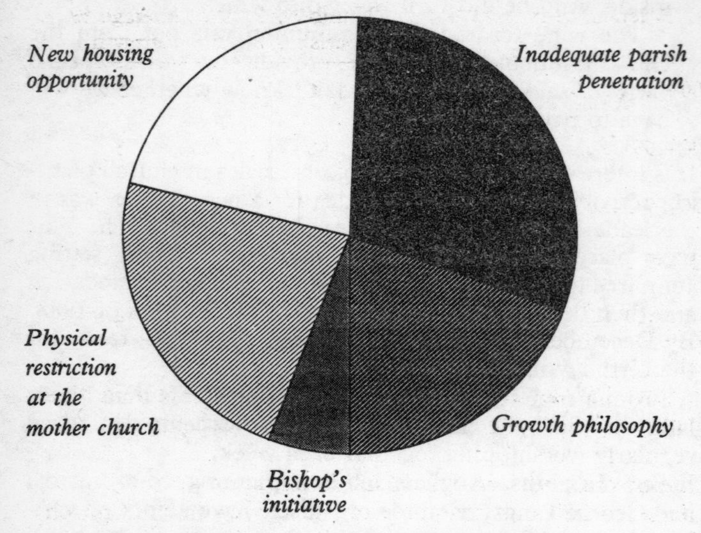

Prime motivations in Anglican church planting

linked to congregation size. In our case, by starting two small congregations which began with fewer than forty, the total number of those attending on Sunday mornings grew from around 200 to around 400 as a result of this strategy.

But although this strategy may work for a few years, there are few parishes which have the physical space for more than two or three new congregations. There is a growing pressure to burst out of the parish boundaries. A message needs to be sent loud and clear to the Church of England Synod that a complete change in thinking is vital if the new wine is not to burst out of the old wineskins and

Table 1 Church growth in Sheffield diocese 1982–88

Attendance in 1982	Number of parishes	Average % growth
200+ .... very large	6	5
100–199 .... large	40	5
50–99 .... medium	70	13
20–49 .... small	49	18
0–19 .... very small	23	34

be lost. Part of this message may be found later in this chapter when we consider denominational drawbacks.

Church planting beyond parish boundaries

The second type of church planting activity in the Church of England goes across the parochial boundaries to a neighbouring parish. Examples of this are pitifully few, but there are some. In 1985 John Irvine, who was working as a curate at 1000 strong Holy Trinity Brompton, led a team of 100 from that congregation across parish and deanery boundaries to St Barnabas' near Shepherd's Bush. This was possible because of three factors. First, the bishop had been enthusiastic in inviting him to the new work and had been wide open to the initiative. Second, the small congregation at St Barnabas', of some fifteen, that were to be 'moved in on' had had to accept radical changes that were presented to them prior to the move for their agreement. They had in fact been most positive and open, entering fully into the new church life with none leaving 'in a huff'. Some had in fact been praying to be 'rescued'! Theirs had been a terminally ill situation with so few worshippers in so large and expensive a building. Third, there was the vision of the home church, Holy Trinity Brompton, to 'give of its best'.

This involved sacrificially giving not just of 100 of the congregation, but of 100 leaders with their financial commitment.

For these three factors to be working together is rare. Happily more and more churches are catching the vision to win more people by planting churches. The numbers may need to be scaled down for many readers from sending 100 to sending twenty, but a growing group of churches from all denominations and streams want to do this. For a bishop to enthuse about such an initiative is, sadly, rare. For a dwindling congregation to be glad to become part of an implanted group in their own building is even rarer. But it does happen, and I venture to suggest should happen wherever there is apparently terminal decline. Under John Irvine's leadership the 100 who came have grown to over 300 in three years.

Denominational drawbacks [mainly for Anglicans]

The Church of England is behind the Baptist Union in halting its decline: the Baptists turned the corner between 1980 and 1985, and thereafter saw a slight growth in membership. Figures released for 1990 show, for the first time since the second world war, a very slight increase in Church of England membership, as well as an increase in those accepted for ordination. Time will tell whether this check in the decline will change into significant growth.

Part of the answer will lie in the ability of church planting parishes to continue to grow beyond their boundaries. This is the first difficulty confronting the growing Church of England church today. In our own case, if we were free to plant **beyond our parish boundaries**, we should already have done so. In many cases where a request has been made, it has met with a flat refusal. This happened for John Aldis of Holy Trinity, Leicester. John led a flourishing, growing city centre church which is outgrowing its accommodation. On two occasions he applied to take over redundant or nearly redundant churches and on a third to start a new church. But in all cases he has been stopped by diocesan authorities as the centres are outside his parish. Their response has been to greatly enlarge the present building but they still feel they must plan to plant churches. Perhaps partly because of these frustrations, John Aldis has now moved to Hong Kong!

What is behind the bishops' and archdeacons' reluctance even to consider breaking up the boundaries seems to be a desire to maintain a mixture of middle, high and low churches and not upset the balance. This amounts to a death wish as it is generally only the evangelical wing of the church that is growing.

Among various statistics confirming this was an analysis which appeared in 1990 of Church of England growth in the Sheffield area between 1982 and 1988. The growth in adult attendance for the diocese as a whole was 14%. But that growth was unevenly spread: Table 2[1] gives a comparison of congregational growth between parishes of different churchmanship.

Table 2 Church growth in Sheffield diocese 1982–88

	Evangelical	Catholic	Middle and other	Total
Number of parishes	42	41	110	193
Total attendance '82	3968	2956	6865	13,789
Total attendance '88	5446	2892	7391	15,729
% growth '82 – '88	+37	−2	+8	+14
Average congregation size '88	130	71	67	81

The difference between the evangelicals and the others is so great that it can almost be said that growth in the diocese as a whole is restricted to evangelical parishes. In 1989 Clifford Longley, writing in *The Times*, asserted that the only hope for the Church of England was that the evangelicals take it over! These statistics show why he proposed this, in his view, 'unhappy solution'.

A second reason for the reluctance of those in authority to encourage church planting as a strategy is the desire to maintain a distinctly 'Anglican' approach to worship. It is as if not too many new churches are wanted because they are rather unanglican. I know a man who, on being offered a particular post, was warned by those in authority that they should 'be taking a close interest in the progress of your work there in order to be assured that the style of ministry of the church observes an Anglican ethos.' Here the preoccupation is with 'style' and 'ethos'. Where was the concern for the thousands not coming anywhere near the church and not caring about its ethos either, but who were bound to an eternity without God? Similarly, I was once asked by an Anglican leader after a long description of the birth, struggle and then growth and conversions in our new community church, 'Yes but, when you celebrate the Eucharist: what do you wear?' My wife suggested that the best answer would have been: 'Clean underwear every time!'

The Church of England's authorities need to be careful lest in their desire to maintain 'ethos' and 'style' they miss completely the breath of the Holy Spirit's life as it blows past them.

Taken in a more generous light, there may be a concern here not to throw out hundreds of years of wisdom and depth in a desire to be trendy. This was expressed by George Carey, now Archbishop of Canterbury. In an article in the *Church of England Newspaper* recommending church planting, he adds this caution:

There is a tendency for church planting groups to assume

they know best what is liturgically best for that area and, sometimes, out of the window goes any recognizable Anglican liturgy with the incumbent who, unrobed and in open-necked shirt, introduces the choruses in front of the now universal overhead projector . . . I am saying we must not supplant Anglican worship for a free-wheeling non-conformist style which owes more to Spring Harvest that the A.S.B.

Some may want to ask immediately: 'Why on earth not?' And those who have been to Spring Harvest may respond: 'To avoid the notices!' Seriously, one can understand the Archbishop's concern to retain the best of the tradition: a liturgy involving elements of worship; confession; intercession; Bible reading; biblical preaching and blessing. Personally, I respect his view and at the same time am glad of his enthusiasm for church planting: 'I am convinced that Church Planting is a mark of vigorous and outgoing Christianity and is a sign of hope for the future', he says.

Later, we shall see that in all the new churches that are being planted we can see some common features, or vital signs: the priority of worship, of covenant relationships, of evangelism and of training. In our experience, all of these can flourish without throwing out Anglican distinctives.

Nevertheless, there will have to be change in style. George Carey himself writes movingly of his running into the brick wall of 'Anglicanism' in his book on renewal, *The Church in the Market Place* (Kingsway, 1989). He describes how he was called to answer complaints from a group of thirty older church members in a chapter aptly entitled: 'You have destroyed my church'. He concludes his reply to them like this:

> 'It must be difficult for many of you to come to terms with new services, strange new songs, guitars and so on. But I want you to observe that the church family is growing isn't it? Isn't that what it is all about? Can we really be happy with a church that is indifferent to the thousands who pass our church doors each day?'

'Our growth consultant thinks the term **church** *sounds outdated.'*

And then he reflects that: 'The difference between us was one of vision. They saw no reason to change – I saw every reason to change . . . One thing we were sure of: we couldn't go back. The Spirit of God was beckoning us forward, and we had to obey.'

I am one of many who saw the appointment of Dr Carey as Archbishop of Canterbury as a prophetic choice for England. I only pray that the vision which he grasped so clearly for the local church might be taught clearly and then caught by the whole Church of England. Without it, it is not an exaggeration to fear that the people will perish.

It may be asked, if there is among Anglican church planters a hesitation about wearing robes and if there is a positive desire to adapt the liturgy of the Church of England, why and in what way can they say that they remain Anglican? My answer is immediately that we submit to our leaders, the bishops, and value highly their pastoral care. Second, we follow with gladness the thirty-nine articles.

Incidentally, it would be good to remember that Article nineteen does not say that 'The church is a congregation with Anglican style' but merely this:

> The visible Church of Christ is a congregation of faithful men, in the which the pure Word of God is preached, and the Sacraments be duly ministered according to Christ's ordinance . . .

This is a very helpful rule of thumb! Moreover, Article thirty-four insists:

> It is not necessary that Traditions and Ceremonies be in all places one, and utterly like; for at all times they have been divers, and may be changed according to the diversities of countries, times, and men's manners, so that nothing be ordained against God's Word.

The great theme of God's word is the love of God for the lost. Jesus left heaven behind him and came and offended the traditions of the church. He expressly forbade men to call other leaders 'Father'. He warned of the dangers of liking to walk around in flowing robes. He commanded his church to be built on the knowledge of God not on ethos. His most effective early church planter laid down the great missionary principle of becoming all things to all men that by all means he might win some. So it is that the new churches are bound to be and look different to the old. This should be encouraged and not criticised.

The Church of England must urgently move away from maintenance into mission. It must not only drop its concern for style and ethos but also for parish boundaries. This is the system by which England is divided up into parcels for which there is a priest who has the 'cure of souls'. Although we respect the pastoral motives for this, it is clear that many of these divisions are arbitrary and unhelpful and unworkable. When one man with a tiny congregation has the cure of 13,000 souls, it is a joke, or it would be if it were not so sad. And yet it is still against the law of the land for another ordained Anglican leader to come in and plant another church to help reach the people! As has been said, one reason given is often 'not wishing to upset the delicate balance of liberal/catholic/evangelical that is the glory of the Anglican middle way'! But to talk like this is to fall into the trap mentioned above of emphasising maintenance not mission. Bob Hopkins quotes the view (see *Church Planting II*, Grove Books, page 21) that the parish boundary at its worst is 'a line drawn round thousands of people to protect them from hearing the Gospel.' David Pytches and Brian Skinner have written an account (unpublished at the time of writing) questioning the usefulness of parish boundaries and citing twenty-seven precedents in which they believe the parish boundaries to have been unhelpful.

My own view is that the Church of England must win its crisis of nerve and dare to do things differently as this millenium draws to a close. It must recognise and rejoice that many of its clergy and thousands of its members are Christians first and Anglicans second. They are more concerned with the lost and how best to win them than with maintaining traditions: who ever dreamt of Anglican ethos in a church meeting in a pub anyway? I long for the day when those in authority will be united in a common quest to win the lost without worrying about the style of Anglican worship; when they will see that a prime means to evangelise our nation will be to plant churches and encourage it without worrying about parochial boundaries. My recommendation is that we scrap them for the ten year decade of evangelism as a trial period and then think again in AD 2000!

Another tragic effect of this emphasis on 'Anglican ethos' and the maintaining of the status quo by parish boundaries is the disincentive to leaders to stay and build a work whose multiplication is limitless. When a curate has planted one new church, he is encouraged strongly to uproot, move and start all over again in a completely new situation. If you wanted to devise a scheme to slow down growth, you could not do better. What would be more helpful would be the encouragement to take a team from your current church to a nearby and needy area so plant from strength, and multiply organically and naturally. When I talk to archdeacons about this, they are quite likely to say (with some notable exceptions!), 'Why not just send the members to another nearby church that is struggling under its present leadership?' This shows a failure to understand the need to plant *in relationship*. The team needs to be in relationship with the leader, and to have confidence in him and so plant from strength. I am also often told that it is not good for a curate's career to stay in the same area or parish! What we need to understand is that we are not talking about career, but about serving Christ and finding the most effective means to win the lost. There is no more effective means for long term evangelism than preparing a team in relationship with a leader, moving in, and planting a church!

In conclusion, we can say that if the only 'planting' strategy currently acceptable in the Church of England is within parish boundaries, then the aspiring planters' strategy should be (i) get ordained, (ii) find a very high population parish, (iii) train teams and leaders and start planting. If however, we can foresee an openness to planting across parish boundaries, then we need (i) to develop training where church planting is happening, (ii) establish communication between training base, areas wanting teams, and supportive bishops, (iii) work with theological colleges in training ordinands to this work, (iv) encourage more leaders with a vision for church planting to get involved with the institutional 'system' with the aim of assisting necessary change, (v) 'boldly go where no one has gone before' – at least hardly any Anglicans in living memory!

A vision for the Church of England

Will any of this ever happen? Part of the answer will lie in whether the church is able to form any common vision for the future.

The prophet was right when he said that without a vision the people perish. A vision is needed now by the Church of England as never before. By 'vision' I mean a statement of long-term purpose. From this, short term strategies and goals can be established. The great reason for the Church of England's perishing, if it does, will be seen to have been a lack of such a vision. As long as its concern (in the absence of a vision) is for 'maintaining the ethos of Anglicanism', it is doomed to grow old and cold and to die. But what if it gets hold of a new vision such as this: 'To bring the nation and all its inhabitants to Christ'? Then it may be able to grasp the nettles of boundaries and ethos and see them as secondary. Then it may be able to form a national strategy to match the vision. Such a strategy would, as in the case of the Baptist Union, include church planting, it would include training leaders for the task, and it would include setting some immediate goals such as those above.

Such a vision is not too deeply buried among the treasures of the Book of Common Prayer. Those coming into leadership are told in no uncertain terms what their task is to be. Everyone who is made a priest is set the following 'weighty Office and Charge' at his Ordination Service:

> . . . to seek for Christ's sheep that are dispersed abroad, and for his children who are in the midst of this naughty world, that they may be saved through Christ for ever.

He is also told to, 'never cease your labour, your care and diligence, until you have done **all that lieth in you**, according to your bounden duty, to bring all such as are or shall be committed to your charge, unto . . . knowledge of God'. Any Anglican knows that 'those within his charge' are not just those in the church, but those in the whole community. He is responsible before God for them.

This outward looking emphasis does not stop with the clergy but is even more demanding for the bishops. These all have to answer two key questions:

> Will you be faithful in ordaining, sending or laying hands upon on others? and: Will you show yourself . . . merciful for Christ's sake to poor and needy people and to all strangers destitute of help?

It is certainly possible to see in the charter deeds of the denomination (which is what the Book of Common Prayer seems to be for many) this vision to reach those outside the church. It would be helpful to state this clearly at the highest level and work out a strategy to match the vision. Clergy can then 'do what lies within them to bring people to know God.' One of these things is certainly to plant churches. Bishops can do what they have already promised to do, namely 'be faithful in laying hands upon others', namely church planters. They will take initiative for the sake of 'the poor and needy strangers', namely those outside the church who have no intention of going near the institutional church. For the sake of this promise, they will want to plant new churches, they will allow new churches to look different, to 'enculturate' the gospel, to become all things to all men with the motive of bringing the poor in spirit to know God. They will want strong churches to reproduce themselves to make this easy rather than working against it, enjoying the fact that it will sometimes mean breaking through the parish boundaries for the greater good of enabling all of the people in all the parishes to hear all the gospel.

If this does not happen, I fear for the future of this denomination which I love and to which I am loyal. Statistics from the MARC Europe census taken in 1989/90 show a devastating loss of life. But it cannot be stressed too strongly that there are places of great strength and potential for growth: they should not be squashed, marginalised and ignored. Instead they should be recognised as a great, hopeful sign for the Church of England. Then plans for re-evangelisation through the planting of churches should be prayed through and published with every effort made to back the movement, rather than break its heart.

As churches are planted across the country, the great need is for leaders who can lead a team, impart a vision for this work, and see it come to pass. We now move on to examine the question: who is equal to this task?

6

'Give me a hundred men. . . .'

It is much safer to be in a subordinate position than in one of authority.

Thomas à Kempis

John Wesley said: 'Give me a hundred preachers who fear nothing but sin, and desire nothing but God, and I care not a straw whether they be clergymen or laymen. Such alone will shake the gates of hell and set up the Kingdom of God on earth.' We are in a decade when the timeless truth of John Wesley's words is apparent, and nowhere more so than in the realm of church planting. The character of the leaders of the new churches is of great significance. They do need to fear nothing but sin and desire nothing but God. Stuart Christine, who teaches the new church planters' programme at Spurgeon's College, concluded after his initial research that the single most important factor in the planting of a new church is the calibre of the leader.

Some who read this will be those who sense the call of God to plant churches. Others will be part of a team. All, we hope, will want to pray. This chapter aims at motivating godly praying in order that leaders will not be sloppy and selfish, but will be shepherds after the heart of Jesus the good shepherd who lays down his life for the sheep.

What kind of leaders are needed for this work? We would do well to look at the life of the one who is arguably the first church planter; the apostle Peter.

Leaders looking up

Called by God

First, Peter was plucked out of his normal employment by the voice of Jesus. The church planter needs to know he is called. Peter may have been reluctant and was certainly aware of his shortcomings, but he knew that he was called. I clearly remember the day I heard the call of Jesus to leave my secular employment. I was sitting in a friend's garden where I had gone to seek the Lord, and as I was reading the words of Jesus I knew, with a peace and a joy which passed understanding, the call of God. **Pray** that the Lord of the harvest would send out labourers into his harvest field. The church planter needs to be a strong, visionary leader with a clear sense of call, not necessarily a nurturer or pastor, although these gifts may be present to a lesser degree.

Open to God

One day Jesus himself was moved to bless particularly Simon son of John. You can almost hear the excitement pouring out of the Master as one of his pupils gets the hang of something he's been teaching and modelling for the past year. That 'something' is the precious, so-seldom-found art of listening to God and hearing him speak. The conversation goes like this:

Jesus: Who do people say the Son of Man is?
Peter: Some say John the Baptist; others say Elijah; and still others, Jeremiah or one of the prophets.

Jesus: But what about you? Who do you say I am?
Peter: You are the Christ, the Son of the living God.
Jesus: Blessed are you, Simon son of Jonah, for this was not revealed to you by man but by my Father in heaven. And I tell you that you are Peter, and on this rock I will build my church, and the gates of Hades will not overcome it . . .

So many will take advice and consult and spend themselves in getting man's opinion without hearing God. Peter is not a recluse: he is aware of what people think. But he is open to God and not afraid to follow what God says. In this case, the revelation is the greatest of all: that Jesus is the Christ. In the next breath, Jesus adds further information, namely that he, Jesus, is the one who will build the church – comforting news for the church planter! **Pray** that leaders are open to God's voice. Peter not only hears it on this occasion but several times in the future, as the book of Acts shows.

Teachable spirit

The fact that Peter heard God's voice about one thing does not stop him arguing with Jesus about the next, namely Jesus' intention to go to the cross. 'Never, Lord! This shall never happen to you!' Peter blurts out. When Peter got it so resoundingly wrong at Caesarea Philippi in telling Jesus not to go to Jerusalem under any circumstances, he received the rebuke to end all rebukes: 'Out of my sight, Satan!' (Matthew 16:23). The remarkable thing is that Peter accepted the rebuke and was teachable. This is something to **pray** for zealously, that leaders be humble enough to admit when they completely foul things up.

This may be part of the leader's secret history with God. It may be that in the past he has been humbled and had to change his thinking. This is good. There is no need to tell everyone all the details, any more than Peter makes any mention or testimony in his letters about the day he messed it up. But it is there. It has happened. He has received the rebuke and not rebelled and left the group. Beware if a potential leader comes in with dissatisfaction at how he has been treated in a previous group. Rather, **pray** that God would raise up those who are teachable.

In our situation we had an incident – trivial by comparison with Peter's – which illustrates well what may happen when someone has a teachable spirit. After a discussion in a staff meeting about the gifts of the Spirit, I remember one of our church planters announcing firmly that in the church he was planting he would forbid anyone to speak in tongues in public! I was, as a newly arrived curate, somewhat taken aback and went home to lick my wounds. Imagine our laughter and hilarity when the same dear friend began our next meeting by saying he wanted to share something before we began, and went on: 'This morning, as I was praying, the Lord gave me the gift of tongues.' When asked how he now felt about his former pronouncement, he replied without hesitation: 'I would have no problem with the use of this gift in public, with interpretation, in fact I would encourage it!' I tell this because the humility and openness to God of my friend has always been an example to me.

Close to God

In the next moment after Peter has been so firmly put right by Jesus, he has an experience that he is never to forget. You can imagine him telling it to his grandchildren. He writes a letter a few years later when he remembers:

> We were eye-witnesses of his majesty . . . We ourselves heard this voice that came from heaven when we were with him on the sacred mountain . . .

The transfiguration (Matthew 17), recorded here in 2 Peter 1:16–18, is of course a unique event, but it is also part of a pattern for Peter's life which shows he was a man who was close to God. **Pray** that our leaders will be too.

Closeness in family
Paul gives a revealing insight into Peter's ministry when he suggests that Peter's wife accompanied him when he was travelling and church building. Our own experience is that we have never yet planted a congregation without each person who is married getting as clear a call to the work as their partner. I would not go as far as one group which makes 'coupleness and a sense of call in husband and wife' one of their ten non-negotiables for church planters. But if you're married, then I would agree!

A past in the process of healing
Peter's attempt to stop Jesus from going to the cross was not his only mistake. He who had been with Christ when the voice came to him saying, 'This is my Son, whom I love', denied him three times a few months later. But what is challenging is that again Peter did not allow this mistake to separate him and strangle the spiritual life from him. Instead he was still with the group when Jesus came and stood with them in the upper room; he was still there, crucially, when Christ questioned him searchingly. In these encounters, Peter was healed not hardened. We would be foolish to expect leaders not to make any mistakes. But will they be healed and restored and forgiven? **Pray** that they may be people who rely on God's healing and allow him to set them back on the track of feeding the lambs.

Led by God
Peter woke up from a violent dream that was to change everything. From now on, the message would go to everyone and not only to the synagogues. Again, the revelation 'do not call anything impure that God has made clean' (Acts 10) was a unique event in the history of the church. But behind it we see a leader who was available to be led by God to break the mould and to go to a completely new group. **Pray** for the church planter to be led by God. At the time of writing, some of us are wondering whether the call of God is to plant our next church in a local pub. This

may not seem too controversial, but when one of the team leaders is an ex-alcoholic it requires tremendous openness to God to go down a risky and unexpected route!

Action

Leaders need to spend time with God as an urgent priority. I recently shared with our church ten steps on time with God. Here they are.

1. Go to bed earlier.
2. Get up first.
3. Ask the Father which passage(s) he wants you to read in the Bible.
4. Note down clearly what he says and meditate on this.
5. Turn on a worship tape and use it to begin to worship.
6. Ask the Holy Spirit to reveal any unconfessed sin in your life, and confess it thoroughly, noting down any action you are prompted to take.
7. Pray through the implications of what you feel God is saying to you.
8. Keep, and use, lists of those you wish to pray for regularly.
9. Repeat steps one to eight the following day.
10. Find another two people to be prayer partners with you once a week so that some of these prayer burdens can be shared and agreed on and so that you can be spurred on by each other's zeal in prayer.

This list is only a means to an end. Jesus said 'Abide in me, and I in you. As the branch cannot bear fruit by itself. . . . neither can you, unless you abide in me . . .' (RSV). The old preachers used to say: 'Have you found the place of abiding?' I want to ask the reader: 'Have *you* found it?' When we make something like these ten steps our daily discipline, we are aiming for it to be a vehicle through which we meet God and learn to love him and listen to him and abide in him. F B Meyer said: 'The great tragedy of life is not unanswered prayer but unoffered prayer.' And Martyn Lloyd-Jones' view was that 'prayer is the ultimate test of a man's true spiritual condition. There is nothing that tells the truth about us, as Christian people, so much as our prayer life. Everything we do in the Christian life is easier than prayer.'[1] The above steps will, I hope, help to make it a little easier. But, above all, we need the Holy Spirit's help. My conviction is that as we take action, and show that we mean business, we will find that it is at that point precisely that the Holy Spirit comes to help us in our weakness and change everything from a mechanical discipline to an encounter with the living God.

Leaders looking in

All the characteristics listed so far tell of the leader's relationship with God ('looking up'). Peter was also good at 'looking in' to the group around him. He was able to motivate others. Maybe it was because he was close to God that the others respected him. At any rate, some things hint at why he was so good at leading his small group. First, he *served the others* in a practical way: whether it was catching and cooking fish (John 21) or serving at tables (before Acts 6), Peter was not afraid to get his hands dirty with practical, menial tasks. When released from prison he shows how he *relied on others*, by needing to be with the church after release from prison rather than going off and licking his wounds by himself. The church planter must break the mould of self-sufficiency and dare to rely on his or her team.

At this stage, Peter also showed he was *stable in adversity*. Although the worst had almost happened, namely he had been threatened with the same fate as Jesus, he did not falter from the task of planting the church in Jerusalem and then in regions beyond. He joined the church's prayer for boldness to do exactly what he had been told by the authorities not to do. Peter showed his reliance on the body of Christ by *enabling others* to take on leadership as early as possible. In this, he was only doing what he'd seen Jesus do. When a new apostle was needed, he looked for one. When a team to serve was needed, he found one. In church growth terms, he had the ability to 'identify, recruit, train, deploy, monitor and nurture leaders'!

Pray that leaders would make strong relationships with their team, and that by the love they have for one another and the joy experienced, others would come to know God.

Action
In the early days, the team would do well to schedule in whole days or weekends to have fun together, to eat together, to get to know one another, to become family. Time spent like this will not be wasted time. Children will not suffer but benefit. Single people and couples will benefit. Leaders who lead the church into this make a radical choice to break the isolationism of so many evangelical Christian nuclear families and create true Christian community.

Leaders looking out

As well as looking up and looking in, the leader needs to look out. He should have a deep love for the lost. Peter watched Jesus as he looked out over Jerusalem seeing the people like sheep without a shepherd, and he learnt from him. He learnt to see people as individuals with a need of God. He learnt to have compassion. He learnt about his dearest friend and Master's concentration on reaching people with the message of the love of God. So when, after being filled with the Spirit on the day of Pentecost, Peter meets the vast crowds in Jerusalem, he doesn't hesitate to speak clearly.

Even when under arrest, Peter goes on caring for others. In chains he tells the Sanhedrin itself about the one name in heaven by which we must be saved. This is an example to the whole church whose prayers focus outwards. When Peter returns after arrest, they don't pray for healing from the memory of the prison but for the boldness to speak the good news!

Pray that God would make leaders be those who look out with compassion and take steps to speak often to others about Jesus.

Action

One way to test your call to this work is to ask the Lord to help you to lead another person to Christ where you are. I remember 'laying down a fleece' that I would not proceed towards the ordained ministry unless the Lord enabled me to lead another to Christ before a certain date: there is nothing that concentrates the mind as such an agreement with God!

As Peter looked outward, he was able to motivate others to change their perspective too. This is a vital gift. When called to go to the gentiles, he was able to manage the change of understanding that this involved for the whole group. In modern terms, he evaluated who was to be evangelised and was willing to take responsibility to go to them in the work of evangelism. These outward looking gifts are vital, but equally vital is the ability to take others with you. Peter showed this when he did not hesitate to take some of the brothers from Joppa with him on the journey to Caesarea and the house of Cornelius. When conversions occurred it was not Peter who was involved in baptising but his team (Acts 10:48).

In writing these biblical guidelines I have had beside me a list of ten non-negotiables for a church planter as taught by the Vineyard Christian Fellowship. They express in church growth terms much of what has been discovered above:

Non-negotiables for a church planter

1. Strong visionary leader (not nurturer, pastor-type

essentially).
2. Ability to identify, recruit, train, deploy, monitor and nurture leaders.
3. Proven track record under supervision.
4. Indigenous support system/lifeline. Not being out on one's own, but connected to another church, churches, group.
5. Clear written plan to work to (five year ideal).
6. Willing to take responsibility for the church to grow, and not wait for it to happen.
7. Effective gathering techniques with ruthless evaluation.
   - Evaluation of who is to be evangelised.
   - Discerning research.
   - Awareness of danger of attracting nominals rather than the repentant.
   - Creating ethos which fits those to be evangelised.
8. Coupleness. Family strength – sense of call in wife and husband.
9. People able to think and problem solve. Manage change.
10. Certainty of call – Ruthless tenacity – No ego problem – Hard worker.

The pastor's function changes as the church grows.

There are growth barrier points at twelve or thirteen, sixty and 200 people. These call for fresh thinking and approach, and a willingness to change function. Having said that, the main task up to 200 remains a gathering task.

Leaders on the bread line?

Peter left his nets to follow Christ. Then he went back to them. And it is probable that he then left them again, taking his believing wife with him, and lived by the gospel.

'So I'd like to begin a ten-part series on stewardship.'

It is likely that the church planter will soon want to leave his secular employment to devote himself fully to the work. This can put a significant strain on resources. Several solutions are being tried at present to finance the tremendous need for leaders that will increase as church planting gains momentum. Some groups advocate leaders working part-time to finance their pastoral responsibilities. Others gain an income from a team of supporters not necessarily in their new church. Others have set up one-year and two-year training courses in church planting, encouraging those being trained to pay for the privilege and so contributing to the financing of church planting, as well as providing workers in training. Others have paid their full-time church planters a proper salary but have felt that there is a limit to the number of times that this may be possible.

In the end, leaders will be supported in the same way as they always have been: by winning people to Christ, who then begin to tithe their income in order to support and set free their leaders for full-time work in the church. In the meantime, as the new church gets established, it will quite obviously not be self-supporting. Church planting leaders may have to go back to secular employment for a time to finance the new work. Ideally this will not be necessary if those who send them have a vision for and support the work financially. But I know of several people who having been in full-time Christian work have been prepared to get a secular job for a time, until the new church was able to support them. For example, this occurred at the start of the new Vineyard churches in England, but there is of course biblical precedent in the case of the tent making Paul! **Pray** that God would inspire leaders to be bold and also to be flexible in the area of finances. May they take realistic action as well as being open to and expectant for the provision of God.

Priorities for new churches

Having seen the motive for and mechanics of church planting, as well as documenting some current initiatives, we turn to the following question: if you're starting a church, what kind of church is desirable? The Bible tells us it's a building not made with hands, but what will it look like? Four clearly identifiable characteristics which I have found in all the new churches – worship, fellowship, evangelism and training – are discussed in the chapters that follow. The chief cornerstone is Christ. The preaching of Christ and the need for men and women to be born from above, I assume. But upon this foundation, what is to rise? What will the main rooms look like? Let's look first at priority number one of these new churches: the call to worship.

7

Worship:
Finding the missing jewel

But headlong joy is ever on the wing.

Milton

There is more healing joy in five minutes of worship than there is in five nights of revelry . . . I say that the greatest tragedy in the world today is that God had made man in his image and made him to worship him, made him to play the harp of worship before the face of God day and night, but he has failed God and dropped the harp. It lies voiceless at his feet.

A W Tozer

'You just go off and have a love feast with the Lord.'

These words were spoken to me with a strong American accent. I've often reflected how I might have reacted in my early days as a Christian to such advice. Initially, I would have been embarrassed or offended. Certainly, I would have felt this was just not British: in short, I simply would not have understood. But in 1976, when Jean Darnall gave me this advice, I knew exactly what she meant and I knew that what she recommended was exactly what I wanted to do. I had become a Christian when leaving Oxford University through reading the Bible and being convinced that the New Testament documents were reliable. It was an intellectual assent to the logic of the evidence and a response of the will to the call of Christ. At the same time, I had a great admiration for Jesus. He seemed to answer every question I had ever asked and to have lived a life far above everything I knew was to be aimed at. Reading the Bible was a fascinating experience but prayer was hard, and churchgoing and worship were also something to be lived through until the time came for the sermon, which I relished.

At this time I began, having been converted through reading the gospels, carefully to read the book of Acts and discovered there a level of Christian effectiveness of which I knew very little. I began to see the key to this as being the fullness of the Holy Spirit. I read in Acts 1 how Jesus promised the Holy Spirit to the disciples so that they might be witnesses. I read in Acts 2 how the Holy Spirit came upon the church, resulting in the disciples declaring the wonders of God. I saw the disciples again consciously filled with the Holy Spirit (Acts 4) resulting in them speaking the word of God boldly. I reflected that I was not sure if I had ever been filled with the Holy Spirit, let alone spoken the word of God boldly. I began to pray that a similar confidence might come to me. In Acts 8, I saw that for the converts in Samaria, although wonderfully converted and delivered from evil (v 7) and baptised (v 12), there was still something missing. We read that the apostles in Jerusalem sent Peter and John down to them and 'when they arrived, they prayed for them that they might receive the Holy Spirit, because the Holy Spirit had not yet come upon any of them; they had simply been baptised into the name of the Lord Jesus. Then Peter and John placed their hands on them and they received the Holy Spirit.'

Broadly speaking, there are two main interpretations to this text. One is that the 'disciples' were not Christians yet ('sub-Christians' as Michael Green puts it) and that the apostles were involved in their conversion. The other is that they were Christians but they received at this point more of the Holy Spirit, they were filled with the Spirit 'as at the beginning.' I see the second intepretation as being the interpretation suggested by the text. Verse 12 says: 'They believed Philip as he preached the good news of the kingdom of God and the name of Jesus Christ [and] they were baptised.' It would be hard to find a more succinct description of conversion. When the apostles came down, they felt there was 'something more' for them and proceeded to lay hands on them that they might receive it.

Reading on in the book of Acts, I was fascinated to see that the experience of Cornelius and his household in Acts 10 was different. Here it was while the first presentation of the news about Jesus is being given that the Holy Spirit was poured out on the Gentile listeners causing them to speak in tongues and praise God (v 47). Evidently the Holy Spirit was not predictable in the order of his action, but his presence was welcomed and anticipated by the apostles. It is such an expectancy that prompts Paul's question to the Ephesian disciples in Acts 19. Here he asks them, 'Did you receive the Holy Spirit when you believed?' implying that it is possible to believe without receiving the Holy Spirit. Later, as Paul prays for the disciples at Ephesus and lays hands on them, they have a similar experience to the household of Cornelius, namely they speak in tongues and prophesy. Whether the Ephesian disciples were Christians or not before Paul's arrival – and the development of the story suggests that he finds they were not – Paul's initial question still assumes that it is possible to be a believer in Jesus without receiving fully the Holy Spirit. This complements the 1 Corinthians 12:3 text: 'No-one can say, "Jesus is Lord," except by the Holy Spirit.' The fact is that disciples then and now may well 'have the Holy Spirit' and yet not have 'received the fullness' of the Holy Spirit.

Commenting on these passages, the great Anglican theologian Griffiths Thomas says this:

> There are those today who may be said to be living as though Pentecost had never taken place. Historically, they are on this side of it; spiritually, they are on the other. We can see this clearly in the story of the men at Ephesus (Acts 19) who had not heard of the gift of Pentecost even though they were living many years after that event. Nowadays, similarly, people know about the Holy Spirit, but have never entered fully into their inheritance in Him.[1]

This was the conclusion I could not avoid in the months after becoming a Christian. My response was to seek God to be filled with the Spirit. I used to sit in my living room with my mouth open, eyes raised to heaven waiting for something to happen to give me this new boldness and this ability to speak in tongues which seemed often to accompany the events in Acts. Nothing happened, except that after a few minutes I checked that no one had come into the room to observe such antics! It was not until I was at a conference at which Jean Darnall was speaking that I saw the need to ask others to pray for me. As she and one other laid their hands on me, I leant on their faith, and I began to speak in a new language words of praise to God. After some time Jean advised me in the words above to go out and be alone with God and express my renewed affection for him. I went and sat in a field and experienced that great bubbling up of love for the Father and for Jesus which I expressed alternately in English and in this new language which I did not understand but which I knew was to be addressed to God and which built me up as I used it. Since that day, there has been a new confidence in witnessing to others about the truth of the gospel. And there has been a song of praise to Christ on my heart. The result has been a hunger to worship God and express love and affection in song and words. There has been a priority of worship.

Barriers to worship

Before this experience, several barriers to worship were present that prevented me from entering fully into the presence of the Father and into the inheritance that Paul expresses so movingly in Ephesians 1. Above all there was poor theological understanding, and little expectation. As the Holy Spirit filled me, the barriers came tumbling down. Broadly speaking, barriers to worship fall into two camps: barriers for individuals and barriers for whole churches.

Personal barriers

First, the barrier is often a lack of theological understanding that the Spirit-filled life as described in the book of Acts is to be anticipated as the experience of believers today. From this flows a lack of expectation. Careful teaching and study of the scriptures is a good battering-ram for this barrier. Second, there may have been severe emotional damage in the past: broken or spoiled relationships with loved ones or with church leaders that have led to unbelief and lack of expectation that God would pour his Spirit into our lives. He will for everyone else – so we say – but not for us. To be aware of how our past can affect our present and to pray with others for healing can be vital. Third, the barrier often has to do with an absence of seeking. James says, in his letter, that we have not because we do not ask. To begin to call out to God to fill us with his Spirit that we might know him better is what is needed. If we can ask others to pray with us, so much the better.

Fourth, the barrier will sometimes be past, and unconfessed, sin. I remember at the conclusion of a church house-party, a man asking me for prayer to be filled with the Spirit. He said he had asked many times before, but he needed to tell me something first. What emerged was his addiction to pornography. He could not shake it off. He told me how he had had problems when young and had assumed that upon his marriage, he would break the habit.

To his despair things had got worse. I asked if he had ever told his wife or anyone else about this before and his reply was, 'No'. He then knelt and confessed his sin to God and asked for the forgiveness that is in Christ to be his. I prayed for him to be filled with the Spirit. He was visibly affected and soon began to speak in tongues a stream of praise to God. Here when the sin in the darkness had been brought to the light its power was broken and in this case confession had battered down the barrier.

Often a new convert will receive the fullness of the Spirit at the same time as they profess faith in Christ. But if not, a fifth barrier, both for new and more mature Christians, to asking for more of the Spirit is still fear of man, and fear of the supernatural. Again, careful teaching is important as well as loving discussion of these often irrational fears. To bring them into the open is often to see their power evaporate.

Whenever the Holy Spirit comes more fully into a person's experience, often with the evidence of speaking in tongues, it is to open a door to a fuller life as a worshipper. Where the door remains shut, this kind of openness to God in worship can remain incomprehensible and even irritating. Many of the new churches see this openness to the Holy Spirit's work, and the intimacy that results, as absolutely vital.

Barriers for churches

As well as personal barriers there can be church barriers, such as liturgical practices that militate against any spontaneity in worship. This leads to a deep frustration among so many of the believers in countless churches. Once we have tasted the intimacy of a whole group being with the Father and hearing his voice, there is placed in the believer a hunger for this that will not go away. But so many churches seem unable to make room for such intimate worship. 'We just don't have that kind of liturgy,' is the excuse that is often heard. The irony is that often they *do* have the liturgy although they have not woken up to it. For example, the

Anglican church has in its communion service a structure which is very similar to that which many of the new churches adopt. In this, we find sections on call to worship; confession; praise; reading of scripture and preaching of the word; response to the word; communion; blessing. In the Baptist church, similarly, there is preparation; praise; preaching and prayerful response on most Sundays. What countless new churches have done is to take these helpful headings and develop what goes on under each one in a way that is flexible.

For example, under the heading 'praise' a set of songs that are helpful in leading the congregation into an awareness of the presence of God may be used. Musicians will be sensitive to the mood of the congregation and adapt their material as the service proceeds. As we shall see, this process often brings a congregation to a point of listening to the Lord's voice. Space should always be made for the prophetic gifts of the Spirit as well as for preaching here. In the new churches, ecclesiastical barriers to intimate worship can be broken while retaining the helpful discipline of some liturgical structure. This can and does of course occur in many other churches too, but the new churches may find change occurs more easily and more quickly.

Stages in worship

The goal of expressing praise is to meet with God, in whose presence there is healing and truth and life in all its fullness. Because of the fragmented and busy nature of our lives, there may be certain stages of preparation needed to approach God in this way. Psalm 95:1–8a gives a helpful model for this.

> Come, let us sing for joy to the LORD;
> let us shout aloud to the Rock of our salvation.
> Let us come before him with thanksgiving
> and extol him with music and song.

For the LORD is the great God,
the great King above all gods.
In his hand are the depths of the earth,
and the mountain peaks belong to him.
The sea is his, for he made it,
and his hands formed the dry land.

Come, let us bow down in worship,
Let us kneel before the LORD our Maker;
for he is our God and we are the people of his pasture,
the flock under his care.

Today, if you hear his voice,
do not harden your hearts.

Call to worship

Verses one and two begin with the heartfelt encouragement: 'Come, let us sing for joy . . . Let us come before him . . .' Often when we meet together we are distracted by a thousand thoughts. On a Sunday at family worship, it may be that there has been a rush to get to the service.

On arrival together, it is appropriate to encourage one another saying, as it were, 'Come on friends, let's do what we've come here to do.' At the time of writing, songs such as, 'We are here to praise you', 'Come, let us sing for joy to the Lord', or the old favourite, 'I will enter his gates . . .' are appropriate. The psalmist is saying: Let's get the instruments out and use our voices. He is reminding us of the way we are coming to the Lord. This call to worship is followed quickly by the call to be thankful: 'Let us come before him with thanksgiving and extol him.' As we give thanks, we take our eyes off ourselves and look again to God. This is healing and renewing and should be given time. As we do 'give thanks with a grateful heart' we remember that the weak can be strong again and this can cause us to 'extol' God, which means to praise enthusiastically (from the Latin *tollo* meaning 'praise'). It is often appropriate to give time for spontaneous prayers of thanks from individuals in the congregation. When you first do this it can seem quite a risk and it may take time for fluency to grow, but it is worth it! There are great pragmatic advantages in giving regular opportunities for this, provided the gathering is not too large. It helps each one to take some responsibility for worship. It can be upbuilding to others in the congregation to hear one another give thanks to God. It can also help the leaders to know where the Holy Spirit is at work. Perhaps he is leading the group into intercession; perhaps towards confession; perhaps towards proclaiming strongly the kingdom of God and engaging in spiritual warfare. The sensitive leader needs to watch and listen as well as to lead strongly.

Call to remember

In verses three to five the psalmist reminds us who it is that we are coming to. It is good to spend time remembering and extolling the attributes of God. Songs such as: 'Ascribe greatness . . .', 'Thank you for being . . .', 'All heaven declares', 'You, O Lord, are a great God . . .' are appropriate here. These songs remind us of the deeds and of the character of God, as does the psalmist who sings:

> for the LORD is the great God,
> the great King above all gods.
> In his hand are the depths of the earth,
> and the mountain peaks belong to him . . .

Call to intimacy

At this point in our communion with God a desire for repentance and confession will mingle with a sense of confident expectancy and joy at being a son, a daughter. The psalmist expects a response that is physical as he invites the worshippers:

> Come, let us bow down in worship, let us kneel . . .

Similarly, we may find that arms and faces are raised, or that kneeling is an appropriate response in the congregation. The sense of belonging may inspire tears of joy or of repentance, or both at once as we continue in this intimate engagement, remembering:

> . . . for . . . we are the people of his pasture,
> the flock under his care

Songs such as 'Father God I wonder . . .', 'You are here . . .', 'Lord you are so precious to me . . .' are appropriate here, with lines that express this intimacy.

Leaders need to lead

This bringing of the people of God back to personal thankfulness for their place in Christ is one of the vital functions of worship, and it can take some time. It can, however, occur within seconds of beginning the worship process. This will depend on where a congregation is. If they have been together for a whole day or days in conference or retreat then there is a dynamic already present. If, however, the church has not met mid-week and if, in addition, since their previous gatherings there have been difficulties of relationship, things may take longer. John Wimber has pointed out that other factors are also involved when a congregation, or housegroup meet for worship. Around 25 per cent of those gathered will be distracted anyway; they may be upset by their home situation; concerned by some event which occurred on their way in; confused by the absence of someone they were expecting to see. In short, all kinds of mundane concerns will be encountered as the church gathers. It is good for leaders to be aware of these if only to see that to gather together towards the Lord may take some time.

In all this, the role of the worship leader is important. Traditional models of 'leading the service' may need to be broken. Lay readers or elders who have traditionally been given this job may well not be gifted to lead the congregation in the way described above. Many will need to pray that they might grow into this new role. The way to do this is to be a worshipper at home. It may be helpful to use the structure of Psalm 95 in your quiet time as a pattern for half an hour to an hour or more of worship each day for a while. In public, as in private, leaders need themselves to be worshippers. To see the leader enjoying God can be the single most helpful factor for a congregation to grow in this area. There are many inspiring books on this, of which perhaps John Leech's *Liturgy and Liberty* is currently the most helpful.[2]

At a recent training breakfast I gave our worship leaders the following fifteen practical points – culled from the current literature – which summarise much of what's been said so far:

In private:

1. Be a worshipper yourself.
2. Get into the presence of the Lord.
3. Seek 'vision' or 'direction' for the meeting.

In public:

4. Focus attention on the Lord by worshipping him yourself.
5. Never cajole or criticise.
6. Don't talk too much.
7. Don't introduce too many new songs at once.
8. Don't fall back on too many old ones!
9. Do learn songs in sets (to maintain the 'flow' between songs) that are sung directly to God.
10. Downplay mistakes and ignore distractions, being aware that worship will ebb and flow.
11. A standing congregation may be more likely to find full involvement.
12. Try to include some spontaneous expression.
13. Be aware you will need to adjust what you have prepared.
14. Do be sincere and normal; don't get religious.
15. Know when to stop.

The goal of intimacy

There are many effects of worship: we know of the victories

in the Old Testament resulting from the people's obedience to God's instruction to worship him. We know of the prison walls crumbling as Paul and Silas praised their God. But the goal of worship is not to get God to do anything for us (whether this is possible or not). Rather it is to know him personally, intimately. This intimate relationship with God comes from the Holy Spirit. He tells our spirits that we are children of God. Within us, the Holy Spirit cries out, '*Abba*, Father.' Much church planting activity (and much else that is good) flows out of this intimacy with God. Many of the new churches being planted have this aim to be intimate with God. From this intimacy flowed the missionary movement of the church which began in an Acts 13 worship meeting. But the goal of worship is not its effects in mission, but simply to know God personally. This may be hard for western activists to take, but it is our highest purpose: to know God and to enjoy him forever. As a congregation comes before God and gives time to him in praise, they are declaring their understanding that this is their highest purpose and pleasure in life: to know God. This is the long lost 'missing jewel of the evangelical church' (to use A W Tozer's words) which has now been found.

This emphasis on worship is at the heart of the gospel itself. It springs from an understanding of the fact that Jesus came to bring men and women in revolt and in slavery back into intimate loving friendship with God. Through his agony on the cross, he cancelled the debt we owed so that we can live in free relationship again with God. When a person believes this great good news, and the Holy Spirit of Jesus invades his being, he cries out, '*Abba*, Father,' and knows the joy of the unclouded embrace of the Father. This is peace with God and joy in believing. This is a new life of loving adoration for the Father and confidence in being his child. This is being born again to a new hope. The book of Ephesians chapter one lists at least ten benefits of this new relationship, among which we find the fact that the new believer is chosen by God; is counted holy; is blameless; is adopted; is forgiven; has an understanding now of the mystery of God's will for man. But the purpose of all this is summed up in the phrase: 'that we . . . might be for the praise of is glory' (v 12). The apostle Peter has a similar understanding of this primary purpose of the church, when he writes: 'You are . . . a holy nation, a people belonging to God, that you may declare the praises of him who called you out of darkness into his wonderful light.'

In these two summary statements from the apostles Paul and Peter we see the link between being and declaring. Paul says we should 'be for the praise of his glory'. Peter says we should 'declare the praises of him.' There is a link between the giving of our lives to God and the giving of praise to God. Some say that worship means the giving of our lives to Christ, presenting our bodies as a living sacrifice to God which is our spiritual worship (Romans 12:1), and that expressing praise is relatively unimportant. But I would rather say that this expression of worship and praise is in fact vital as the outward sign of an inward grace. The inward grace is that we have been born to a new relationship with God. One outward, visible sign – alongside a daily obedience to God – is the priority given to songs and expressions of worship. When we express our love for someone, if we are sincere, the relationship deepens. By contrast, if we do not express and verbalise it, something is lost.

This fact is well illustrated in the familiar story of the married couple whose relationship was in trouble because the husband never told his wife he loved her. In the end, her uncertainty grew to such a pitch that she expressed it.

Wife:	Listen, I wish you would tell me, 'I love you.' I don't want to complain about our marriage or suggest I'm dissatisfied, but I just do wish that once in a while you'd tell me, 'I love you.'
Husband:	Listen; on our wedding day didn't I say it? Didn't I?
Wife:	Well – er – yes, you did say it then.

Husband: Okay. When the position changes, I'll let you know.

Needless to say, this attitude did not make for a good marriage. The reason? Because love deepens when it is expressed. If we never express personally and intimately our love for Christ, this intimate relationship side of our inheritance in Christ will remain stunted.

Call to listen

Psalm 95 continues: 'Today, if you hear his voice . . .' Often, it is as we become aware of the presence of God that he will speak to his people. Sometimes the presence of God is not accompanied by any particular instruction other than to reveal his holiness and awesome power. This was the case at the dedication of the temple in Solomon's day when simply we read: 'the glory of the LORD filled the temple.' However, when the prophet Isaiah had a similar revelation of the presence of the holy God of Israel, the revelation of the character of God was accompanied by instructions to preach to the unbelieving people. Shortly after the birth of the church, when the leaders gathered together to worship the Lord with fasting, the result was that 'the Holy Spirit said, "Set apart for me Barnabas and Saul for the work to which I have called them." ' How the Holy Spirit spoke at this time is unclear, but it seems reasonable to suppose that it was through a prophecy or exhortation given through another of the leaders.

Today, it is often at times of intimacy in worship that the voice of the Lord will be heard through prophecy, tongues with interpretation, exhortation, or the reading of a scripture that has a particular relevance. A common denominator of many of the new churches will be the regular use of these spiritual gifts, but how can we encourage the worshippers to grow in maturity in their use? Above all, the congregation will hear the voice of the Lord through the preaching, but what kind of preaching is desirable in these new churches? We return to these vital questions in our next chapter, but first we need to complete the stages in worship that Psalm 95 suggests as a model.

Call to obey

After the call to worship, the call to remember, the call to intimacy and the call to listen, comes the call to obey.

> Today, if you hear his voice,
> do not harden your heart as you did at Meribah . . .

The psalm refers back to the dreadful moment when the children of Israel, set free from Egypt, quarrelled with Moses about the lack of water, saying: 'Is the Lord among us or not?' It is one of the greatest tragedies of the church in the west today that there is a similar grumbling and hardening of heart, so that the word of the Lord is simply not heard; and if heard, then it is not obeyed. Certainly, one of the prime reasons for powerlessness is lack of obedience. It is futile to sing to the Lord with enthusiasm, thank him for his personal love, make room for prophecy that is specific and heartwarming, hear the challenging exposition of the Bible if in the end the call is simply not obeyed. And yet many of these new churches have to confess they find themselves in precisely this position. The word of the Lord may have to do with faith in God that cuts people free from besetting depression, it may have to do with simple lifestyle or it may have to do with befriending non-Christians. Very commonly, it is simply not obeyed.

With the new churches as with the old, without an obedience that means a radical change in lifestyle, powerful words from God will fade, the membership will become fat and complacent and another generation will not hear the gospel because of the disobedience of the church.

How then can we encourage obedience? First by focussing attention carefully on what God says. This may mean repeating from week to week a message until it is obeyed. One practice we have followed for some time in mid-week housegroups is to follow up and apply further what has been taught on Sunday. This means that the congregation is not hearing several messages at once but one at a time; and it also makes it possible for members of the congregation to challenge and encourage one another to be obedient. But for many people the problem is further back than that. The word of God is simply not being heard. The gifts of the Spirit are not expected and the preaching is weak. We return now to a fuller discussion of how to encourage these vital ministries.

8

Worship: Hearing the voice of the Lord

We can only give to Him what we receive from Him, and when we receive living bread and living water from the house of bread, there is no other possible response than worship. Why is the worship life of so many Christians so poverty stricken? One reason is they have drawn so little and therefore can give so little. The more the Word of God becomes part of our lives, the more of the Word we will pour out to our Lord.

Campbell McAlpine

As the congregation draws near to God the expectation is to hear his voice, and this should be seen as part of intimate worship. The two main means in the New Testament for a congregation to hear the word of the Lord were preaching and prophecy. When we plant new churches we will do well to give careful attention to both and to make room for both.

Prophecy

Beginning to prophesy
It is clear that prophecy was part of the experience of the

people of God in the Bible (see Numbers 11:20, 1 Samuel 19:20, Joel 2:28, Acts 2:18; 15:22; 19:6; 21:9, 1 Corinthians 11:4–5; 12:28; 14:1 and 24, Ephesians 4:11, 1 Thessalonians 5:20 for just a sample of instances). But what of this ministry today? Are there steps through which we can begin to learn again what was so clearly a part of the New Testament church's experience? It seems clear that there is a distinction between the one who is a prophet and those who from time to time prophesy. When someone is regularly and edifyingly prophesying with fruitful results, then it may be he will become known to have the ministry of a prophet. But how can we even begin to prophesy occasionally? The answer to this question lies in consistent teaching, seeking, surrender and testing.

Consistent teaching

In encouraging the use of prophecy we need consistent teaching as regards what it is. When we examine prophecy in the Bible we soon conclude that it can be predictive (telling about the future) or proclamatory (telling about God) or both. This will free people from thinking they need to know the future before they prophesy. For further teaching, we need to look at 1 Corinthians 14 where Paul speaks most clearly about the gift of prophecy. In verse three he says, 'Everyone who prophesies speaks to men for their **strengthening, encouragement** and **comfort.**' In verse 24 and 25 he adds this: 'If an unbeliever . . . comes in . . . he will be **convinced** by all that he is a sinner . . . the secrets of his heart will be laid bare. So he will fall down and worship God, exclaiming, "God is really among you!" ' Paul gives four words describing the effect of prophecy: Vine's expository dictionary gives the following definitions for each one.

Strengthening (NIV) is from the Greek word *oikodomeō*, meaning – 'edify; to build a house; promoting spiritual growth; suggesting such spiritual progress as the result of patient labour.'

Encouragement (NIV) is from the Greek word *paraklēsis*, meaning – 'encourage; a calling to one's side; consoling, encouraging; advocate, pleading one's cause.'

Comfort (NIV) is from the Greek word *paramuthion*, meaning – 'comfort; speaking closely, tenderly to one who is near; consolation with great tenderness.'

Convinced is from the Greek word *elenkhō*, meaning 'convince; convict; usually suggests putting a person to shame; telling someone his fault is in view.'

The first three words have to do with building up, and the last with tearing down. Some prophecy should therefore be painful to receive, particularly to the outsider, but by no means all. Sometimes much prophecy is criticised as seeming to be fairly sugary and banal, and at times of course it may be. But the apostle in verse three uses words that suggest that much true prophecy is positive, tender, consoling, and patiently upbuilding. So we can ask our congregation: 'Do you want to console those who are broken hearted? Do you want to build up tenderly lives that have been torn apart with pain?' Usually the answer is Yes, and if so, then we can say: 'Earnestly desire to prophesy.' The next question is likely to be: but how?

Consistent seeking

One prophet who so remarkably combines a rebuking with a strongly consoling side to his ministry is Isaiah, and in a beautiful passage (Isaiah 50:4,5) about God's communication to man he says this:

> The Sovereign LORD has given me an instructed tongue,
> to know the word that sustains the weary.
> He wakens me morning by morning,
> wakens my ear to listen like one being taught.
> The Sovereign LORD has opened my ears,
> and I have not been rebellious;
> I have not drawn back.

It seems from this that the way this prophet learnt to prophesy was as the Lord wakened him morning by morning. The way he gained 'the word that sustains the weary' was not like a bolt from the blue, but through patiently listening to God morning by morning. For the Christian today it is obvious that it is in time spent alone with God in reading the Bible, meditating on the words of Jesus, listening to God, that we will be impressed by particular truth. When we then find ourselves confronted by the weary who need sustaining, both in personal conversation and in public worship alike, we have this reservoir to draw on. We may well find that what we are saying comes to others as God's word with prophetic power, as it has already so come to us.

The next verses in Isaiah 50 show that the passage is pointing forward to Jesus:

> I offered my back to those who beat me,
> my cheeks to those who pulled out my beard . . .
> Therefore I have set my face like flint.

Clearly, the writer is also looking forward to the day when the Word of God will become flesh and live among us. The application of the verses to Jesus himself reminds us of the pattern of life of the Master. He himself rose early to talk with his Father and listen to his voice in prayer. There also, in the early morning prayer time, Jesus heard the word that would sustain the weary he met during the day. If this was his rule of life, should it not also be ours? So these passages encourage us to see that one way to begin to prophesy is to listen to God expectantly as each day begins. This has the value of removing prophecy from the realm of the mysterious and placing it firmly in the practical. And the same process can be true of the other spiritual gifts.

Consistent surrender

As well as biblical teaching, the example of leadership is vital in encouraging the use of spiritual gifts. In the new churches, by definition, the leaders must be those who are prepared to take risks. One great risk they have already taken is to plant a new church: after all, it may not survive!

'I know it's early, Pastor, but I figured you'd be up praying.'

It is also important for the leaders to take the lead in public worship in prophesying or in publicly speaking in tongues, or in the use of the word of knowledge. This can be a very traumatic experience as the leader risks looking stupid when things (as he fears) may go wrong. There is no way to avoid taking these risks. Christ has called us to step out by faith and this is one very small way in which we can do so. It means that the leader is not afraid to wait on God, and is not afraid to encourage the whole congregation to wait with him. These are moments of some tension, but if he has a team looking for the same thing, they are at least not lonely moments.

I remember clearly one of the first times I gave a word of knowledge. It was at a meeting at Trinity College, Bristol. This was my theological college and I was anxious to be sound and reliable. However, within minutes of starting the meeting (or so it seemed) I had invited someone with a severe pain in the head to come forward. There was no response and the meeting continued on another tack until a man came from the back of the room with a story about how he had, in the pitch black night, walked straight into a lamp post on his way home the night before: hence the severe head pains. As we prayed for him it was clear that the Holy Spirit was touching him powerfully, and he began to speak in tongues for the first time. He was not only healed but wholly overcome with joy as well. Such stories abound and are important in that often the first thing that needs to be broken in us is pride, fear of men and the need to be in control. Instead we need to learn to commit our minds to God and listen to his voice and then speak in obedience to him. In my brief experience, to do so is well worth the risk involved!

Consistent love

Sometimes, far less risk is involved: a prophecy will simply be an expression of God's love for the congregation. The following is recorded by Bruce Yocum in his thorough book, *Prophecy*:

> Yes my people, my beloved children, come into my presence, be with me today.
> Worship me for I am here among you.
> Open your hearts to me: let me fill you with my love.
> Let me clothe you in my righteousness as you bow before me.
> I am the Lord your God, the mighty God of all.
>
> Be assured of my love for you.
> Be assured that I am with you.
> Open now your hearts to me; give your love to me.
>
> Move with me; as I bid you, come.
> Know the love of your God.
> And know the life of his people.
> Indeed, I am with you.[1]

Here, this contribution is similar to many given as a church begins to worship. It helped the whole congregation realise the affection of their heavenly Father in a fresh way for that day: as such it was encouraging, strengthening and was not to be despised!

Consistent testing

Implicit in the anecdote about the sore head was the need to test the utterance. Bluntly: was there someone in the meeting who responded and benefitted? As we encourage the gifts of the Holy Spirit, and especially prophecy, we need to know how to test them. As we do this, we can encourage consistently those in whom this gift is developing, and perhaps see some move from prophesying to having a mature ministry as a prophet. Many have written on testing prophecy and really what needs to be done is common sense. We need to:

1. **Test the content**: Does what is said glorify Christ? Is it biblical?
2. **Test the appropriateness**: Does what is said fit in to what God is saying to others in the body? This may be in a particular meeting or over a period of time.
3. **Test the spirit**: Is it spoken in love? Does the prophecy build up, console, comfort? Does it convict or does it condemn? There is no need for haranguing, badgering, judgmentalism or excessive emotion.
4. **Test the person**: Is Jesus Lord of the speaker's life? (He doesn't have to be perfect, but is he clearly under God's authority?) Is he submissive to church leaders? A sign of a false prophet is a drawing away in independence from the main body of the church. Is the person growing in maturity or not? Is there a hunger for God and for purity and holiness?
5. **Test the fruit**: As time goes by, are people being helped by what is said? Most importantly, is what is said coming true?

In all this, we need to have the goal of enabling prophesying to mature. This means that testing must be done with an attitude of love and helpfulness. The fact that one prophecy does not come true does not mean you are dealing with a false prophet: 'It is possible for a true prophet to prophesy from the flesh or in the excitement of a moment . . .' says John Wimber.[2] In addition, the prophecy may be of mixed value, having one part God's truth and two parts human enthusiasm. Leaders must make the effort to consult and correct and encourage so that what may begin in childishness can grow to maturity. Bruce Yocum's book, *Prophecy*, contains this conclusion: 'As soon as we speak of prophets, people are immediately worried about false prophets. On the contrary, it seems that we should pray for prophecy! The problem now is an absence of prophets. It seems that the Holy Spirit is raising up prophets in our midst. We should be attentive. The community can judge the worth of prophecy after it happens. BUT LET IT HAPPEN FIRST!'

And God appointed . . . prophets

We live in a day when not only the gift of prophecy but also the ministry of the prophet is being restored to the church. As I write, the invitation has gone out to a thousand mainstream church leaders to attend a London conference, 'to equip church leaders who desire to develop the gift and ministry of prophecy.' The signs are that more and more will be heard of this gift as we approach the end of the millenium. Broadly speaking, prophecy for Britain falls into two camps: for the nation and for the church. For the nation, what is being said is that unprecedented revival is coming and exceeding any ever seen before. People report visions of stadia filled to overflowing with vast crowds: people flocking to hear evangelists preach about Jesus and heal the sick. But preceding this, for the church, unprecedented unity such as is necessary to cope with the vast numbers flowing into the kingdom has been seen. With greater privilege comes greater responsibility. And so repentance and a purging process within the church as she seeks the face of the Father and becomes purified with a longing for holiness is to come. As so often when something good is being restored to the church, its arrival is not without controversy.

For these prophetic pronouncements, exactly the same process of checking and testing is appropriate. At the time of writing, all I can do is to encourage the reader not to despise prophecies, but to test everything, pay attention, look and see whether these things come to pass: test the fruit.

Returning now to the context of a church planting team, it will not be such national pronouncements that are being sought: rather it is the expression of words from God that build up the individuals listening. What is appropriate is first to desire to love your local church; second, get alone with God and see what he wants to say to the church; third, to begin to express this in your housegroup: 'I feel what God is saying is . . .' Fourth, if this has been found to be fruitful, to begin to prophesy in your congregation's meeting, aiming to 'speak to men for their strengthening, encouragement and comfort.' In this way, the new church will recover one of the prime New Testament gifts to build up the church.

Preaching

And God appointed . . . teachers

The apostle Paul, while encouraging the Corinthians earnestly to desire spiritual gifts, especially that they might prophesy, has another conviction about what will build up the church, namely, the preaching and teaching of scripture. This he expresses forcefully to Timothy when he says, in 1 Timothy 4:13,

> Until I come, devote yourself to the public reading of Scripture, to preaching and to teaching.

It is important to value highly this provision from God to build up the church. We note that it came top of the apostles' agenda when the members of the brand new church 'devoted themselves to the apostles' teaching' (Acts 2:2). In Acts 6 we find the apostles cutting out other responsibilities to make time to 'devote themselves to prayer and the ministry of the word' (Acts 6:4). When the new church is planted, this careful explanation and application of the Bible will, above all things, bring life to the congregation.

It is good to allow the word of God to dominate and determine not only the content but also the structure of what we preach. So often the preacher has an idea that he feels strongly about, and he then casts around for a scripture that seems to fit his message. This may succeed for a week or two but in the end is bound to be as banal as the preacher's brain, returning with monotony to well worn paths and well worked passages. By contrast, the Bible tells us it should be the other way round: the Bible text should be the starting place for our teaching. 'Let the word of Christ dwell in you richly as you teach and admonish one another' (Colossians 3:16).

I remember learning this lesson painfully when as a new curate I came to the weekly staff meeting in Cranham. When the time came for constructive criticism of my sermon, my friend Hartmut Kopsch remained resolutely silent. I pressed him for his view and he eventually gave it: 'All very true and orthodox, Charlie, but completely lacking in power.' When pressed as to why he thought this was, he got on to what I later found was a cause he would die for. 'You did not expound the words of scripture. You see, it's the words that have the power, not our ideas. It's the divinely inspired holy revelation that brings life. Our job is to be dominated by and subject to that and to be a mouthpiece for Jesus again to speak through us to his people.' Although depressed about my sermon, this was a life changing day for me. I had been four years at an evangelical theological college but no one had ever put it like that to me.

This is a truth that Dick Lucas and the Proclamation Trust in London have effectively and consistently brought to the church in the last years. Dick has had a ministry to

'Of course, there may be other interpretations.'

businessmen for many years. Each week hundreds of high powered pin-striped suited punters press into St Helen's, Bishopsgate to hear his painstaking explanation of the Bible. One company director – then unconverted – whom I took there for the first time one Tuesday had this reaction: 'All my life I have been longing without knowing it to hear preaching like this.' The following week he took his family on Sunday and has been a member of the church ever since. I believe it was the fact that the preaching was truly expository that hooked him. There is a famine of hearing the word of the Lord in the land, but few places where we can confidently expect to hear it. How we need to pray that for each new church planted there will be those who understand this need and whom God has gifted for this task: to let the scriptures speak, and through the scriptures to let Jesus speak.

We may well ask: where shall I begin in teaching a brand new congregation? It is good to remember Spurgeon's call to his students on this subject:

> Of all I wish to say this is the sum; my brethren, preach Christ always and evermore. He is the whole gospel. His person, offices and work must be our one all comprehending theme . . .[3]

When Cranham Community Church started, we began in the gospels, taking the uncomfortable passages with the more familiar, always trying to ask the questions: what did this passage mean for its original listeners, and now what does it mean for us today? Later, I felt there was a need to lay some foundations of understanding as to the doctrine of the church and for several months expounded Ephesians under the title: 'Build your church, Lord.' I can think of no better manual for life in the kingdom than this 'Queen of the epistles'. Balanced with a diet of the gospels, I would look on it as the church planters' manual. When we announced a course of foundation principles for the church, we broke Ephesians down as follows:

Worship
One: our purpose in Christ; to be to the praise of his glory (1:3–14). Two: our inheritance in Christ; to know him (1:15–23). Three: our indebtedess to Christ; saved by grace alone (2:1–22).

Evangelism
One: God's ultimate purpose; to bring everyone together

under one head, even Christ (2:11–22). Two: Paul's calling and his message (3:1–13). Three: Paul's prayer for the Ephesians to be filled with power (3:14–20).

Fellowship
One: the gifts and calling of the Holy Spirit given that we may attain unity and maturity (4:1–16). Two: the language and character of kingdom people (4:17–32). Three: rejecting the flesh and being filled with the Spirit (5:1–21). Four: life in the Spirit in marriage and home and work (5:22–6:9).

Warfare
The armour of God for the fight (6:10–19).

Of course, each passage and theme overlaps. For example, Paul concludes his description of his calling as an evangelist with a great insight about the gospel: 'In him and through faith in him we may approach God with freedom and confidence.' This rightly brings us back to the subject of worship rather than evangelism. In a brand new fellowship Ephesians, carefully preached, will bring the people into intimate knowledge of God and his purposes, which is the goal of worship.

9

All you need is love

Wouldest thou know thy Lord's meaning in this thing? Know it well: Love was His meaning. Who showed it thee? Love. What showed it thee? Love. Wherefore showed it He? For Love . . . Thus was I learned that Love is our Lord's meaning

Julian of Norwich

Genesis tell us that, 'It is not good for the man to be alone,' revealing that we belong together. We have come a long way since then, and one of the greatest stresses in the world today is loneliness. And the church has the answer to it – or has she? Some say that the church has significantly failed to provide a safe 'family', and the result has been that thousands of needy people have drifted through and away to the false substitutes of the world. Some say that it is because the church has neglected, in almost every generation, to create a true fellowship in Christ that we are faced with modern freemasonary or, more recently, acid house or the New Age groups. Dr Mann, a leading American psychiatrist, has written: 'The church has failed me and most of my patients, because it has never discovered the secret of community fellowship.'

Apart from loneliness, there is guilt, broken hopes, illness and emotional despair. When we watch the news it is sometimes possible for a moment to catch the sheer weight of pain under which the world groans. Again and again we need to ask: Where is the church? Where is the true blood-bought fellowship of brothers and sisters who live together and share together as a family to whom the despairing may turn? Where, today, is the church sufficiently aware of the problems behind closed doors in the lonely streets that it is able to offer true community and true family when it is definitely needed?

The plan and power of love

Sadly, church people have often so dismally failed to get along with each other that they are powerless to get along with the needy in the world. Yet God planned it differently. He planned for the church to be a community where people love each other in a way that is irresistably attractive. We see this at the birth of the church where 'all the believers were together', 'all the believers were one in heart and mind . . .', 'they shared everything they had . . .', 'there were no needy persons among them . . .', 'and the Lord added to their number daily those who were being saved' (Acts 2:42–47; 4:32–35).

Before my wife was a Christian, she moved to Cambridge to study and had nowhere to live. Some Christian girls took her to live with them in a tiny flat where she slept on a sofa in the cramped living room. They didn't preach to her, but they did love each other. What a contrast to the previous student flats she'd shared, where it was every man for himself! These Christians served each other, did not fight each other, laughed with one another, and did each other's washing-up! Soon afterwards, Annie became a Christian.

The cost of love

When the decision comes to plant a new church, one of the

great joys that initially the team finds is that of intimacy with one another: a true fellowship. When the team shares one purpose and each member has a similar commitment to sacrifice time and money for it, there can be moments of great joy. The psalmist cried out:

> How good and pleasant it is
>   when brothers live together in unity. . . .
> There the LORD bestows his blessing.

And the team will cry out for joy as well, because we were created for this community, and in a way we have been looking for it all our lives.

However, our experience was that the very week that our new church planting team began to meet, with such rosy hopes, a violent row between two families occurred which resulted in one couple leaving the team and the church. Despite the instability of this couple, the team was badly shaken and many relationships suffered, much misunderstanding continued no matter what was done to clear it up. Since then, despite deep and life changing bonds being formed, some relationships have at times threatened to go badly wrong.

People in the team have hurt one another, usually unwittingly, and have in turn been cold shouldered. Our attempt to be an intimate family has foundered! After this, depression sets in and deep seated anger can take root. And when the same thing happens again, this makes the reaction all the more violent.

At these times, when the dreams of the new church being the embodiment of close affection one to another have disintegrated, members are tempted to ask: Why don't we give up? Is this quest for deeper relationship and trust fruitless?

Even if such a quality of relationship is possible, is it not too painful to achieve? All these questions become acute, and unless we have a clear understanding of what is at stake we may quickly go under and revert to the low expectations for church life that have perhaps characterised our previous experience.

What we are fighting for is something for which Jesus himself took time out to pray for on the night he was betrayed: the unity of believers. This unity is on a level above anything else we can experience: it is Trinity unity. Jesus prayed that we might be one as he and the Father are one. In other words, what we should be aiming for is a trust, respect, sharing, honouring, building up and obeying of one another such as Jesus experienced with his Father. First, we need to gain a vision for this unity. Then we need to see that as Jesus prayed for it, it is possible for it to occur! Third, we need to recognise the power of this unity. Jesus said, 'I pray . . . that all of them may be one . . . that the world may believe.' In other words, it is this unity that will convince the world of the divinity of Christ. Fourth, we need to know our enemy. No wonder Satan would attack the unity of the fledgeling church. When light dawns as to what we are fighting for and why it is so difficult to achieve, sometimes we can break off and laugh with relief and take the steps to reconciliation that, again and again and again seem to be necessary.

The labour of love

Ken Wilson, of the Emmaus fellowship in Ann Arbour, Michigan is not ashamed to give clear step-by-step models for how to pray for relationships that have gone wrong.

Step 1: Admit wrongdoing to yourself. Don't rationalize it, excuse it, or explain it away, but admit it. Take personal responsibility: 'I did it, and it was wrong.' Then renounce it.

Step 2: Confess what you did wrong to the person you wronged. 'Look, I'm responsible for those rumors that have been circulating about you and damaging your reputation. I was wrong to do that.' 'I was wrong' is harder to say than 'sorry.'

Step 3: Ask the person wronged to forgive you, clearly

and explicitly. 'I was wrong. Please forgive me.' 'Love means never having to say you're sorry' is wisdom from below. There is great healing power in the words, 'Please forgive me.'

Step 4: If you are the person wronged, clearly and explicitly extend forgiveness by saying, 'I forgive you.' Not, 'Oh, that's all right,' or, 'Don't mention it,' or other statements that skirt the issue. What is needed is a plain, simple, and straightforward, 'I do forgive you.'

Step 5: Make restitution, if possible. If you've been gossiping about someone, go to those you gossiped to and try to restore the person's reputation. If you didn't live up to your word then do the thing you said you would do but didn't.[1]

Leadership for love

As in all aspects of the new church's life, leaders must lead. We have often found people will nod and agree to the principles but never put them into practice. They were too embarrassed or didn't want to make a mountain out of a molehill. If this is the case, leaders need to do some personal coaching. This means asking: 'Did you ask that person for forgiveness?' 'Well, why not do so? This is how to begin . . .' Coaching also means insisting at housegroup level that if someone makes a commitment to the group and doesn't live up to it that they say Sorry to the group about it. If things never get sensitive and personal, then leaders are probably settling for less than the best. Once reconciliation has happened, it is important not to see it as the end of the process. Often what has gone wrong has happened as a result of lack of communication. Two people have not spoken to each other for months and during that time the sun has gone down day after day upon their anger with each other. Then they meet for half an hour and get reconciled. They may feel at the time very sincere about their forgiveness but if that is all that happens the old feelings of misunderstanding and bitterness can swiftly recur. The solution for this is to get together again soon and reaffirm love and commitment to one another. Again, love and trust deepens and grows when it is expressed.

Healing the bear with the sore head

We have still, in the first months of a new church's life, known some intractable difficulties where one member finds it impossible not to feel betrayed, usually by the leaders. Dietrich Bonhoeffer in his brilliant chapter on community in *Life Together* (SCM) describes precisely this character and his problems:

> Innumerable times a whole Christian community has broken down because it had sprung from a wish dream. The serious Christian, set down for the first time in a Christian community, is likely to bring with him a very definite idea of what Christian life together should be and try to realize it. But God's grace speedily shatters such dreams. Just as surely God desires to lead us to a knowledge of genuine Christian fellowship, so surely must we be overwhelmed by a great general disillusionment with others, with Christians in general, and, if we are fortunate, with ourselves.
>
> By sheer grace God will not permit us to live even for a brief period in a dream world. . . . He who loves his dream of a community more than the Christian community itself becomes a destroyer of the latter, even though his personal intentions may be ever so honest and earnest and sacrificial.
>
> God hates visionary dreaming; it makes the dreamer proud and pretentious. The man who fashions a visionary ideal of community demands that it be realized by God, by others, and by himself. He enters the community of Christians with his demands, sets up his own law, and judges the brethren and God himself accordingly. He stands adamant, a living reproach to all others in the circle of brethren. He acts as if he is the creator of the

Christian community, as if his dream binds men together. When things do not go his way, he calls the effort a failure. When his ideal picture is destroyed, he sees the community going to smash. So he becomes, first an accuser of his brethren, then an accuser of God, and finally the despairing accuser of himself.

Such people are like a bear with a sore head. The first solution is mutual confession of sin and wrong feelings, and this may have to happen again and again with the same people. As it does, there may well be a place for prayer for healing of the emotions. Often strong feelings of mistrust or vulnerability come because of something going badly wrong in another church or as a child. What is needed is prayer for healing. Sometimes we will arrange to meet once a week for five weeks to talk and pray. The aim is to invite the Holy Spirit to reveal what is causing this block to growth and to invite him to heal and restore to wholeness the person in question.

This may seem labour intensive and potentially introverted. But many evangelical congregations are stymied and rendered impotent by a tangled web of relationship difficulties. It does not have to be that way. The new church has an opportunity to start afresh and keep clean and clear and strong relationships. The Bible provides a clear and simple way to clear up the major cause of trouble, and that way is reconciliation. The Bible also suggests the need to work at keeping the unity in the bond of peace. Steps 1 to 5 listed on pages 121 and 122 have helped us again and again in moving toward this aim.

Building for community

My parents

Sunday is a funny day,
It starts with lots of noise.
Mummy rushes round with socks,

And daddy shouts:
'You boys!'

Then mummy says: 'Now don't blame them,
You know you're just as bad,
You've only just got out of bed,
It really makes me mad.'

My mummy is a Christian,
My daddy is as well,
My mummy says: 'Oh heavens!'
My daddy says: 'Oh, hell!'

And when we get to church at last,
It's really very strange,
'Cos mum and dad stop arguing,
And suddenly they change.

At church my mum and dad are friends,
They get on very well,
But no-one knows they've had a row,
And I'm not gonna tell.

People often come to them,
Because they seem so nice,
And mum and dad are very pleased
To give them some advice.

They tell them Christian freedom
Is worth an awful lot,
But I don't know what freedom means,
If freedom's what they've got.

I once heard my mummy say
She'd walk out of his life.
I once heard daddy say to her
He'd picked a rotten wife.

They really love each other
I really think they do.
I think the people in the church
Would help them – if they knew.

Adrian Plass[2]

One of the tragedies of the church is that people come to find true community, but all that there is is pseudo-community in which masked people abound. Scott Peck defines this brilliantly: 'In pseudo-community a group attempts to purchase community cheaply by pretence. It is not an evil, conscious pretence of deliberate black lies. Rather, it is an unconscious, gentle process whereby people who want to be loving attempt to be so by telling little white lies, by withholding some of the truth about themselves and their feelings in order to avoid conflict. But it is still a pretence. It is an inviting but illegitimate shortcut to nowhere.'[3] The poem above provokes an amused response in many of us, but we urgently need to create a safe place in which the mask can be dropped: such a place may be the healing prayer partnership described above, or it can equally well be the properly functioning housegroup.

Housegroups

A vital means to expressing and achieving mutual support in the fight for the kingdom is the small group. Many such groups founder through lack of goals or through poor leadership. We have found it important to limit drastically the goals for the homegroup to that of mutual support and prayer. The most frequently asked question therefore is simply: 'Where are you at?' Sufficient time needs to be given to listening to the answer and then to prayer and ministry to meet the needs another member has. All else flows from this goal of building one another up.

Our theological understanding is that our top priority should be to worship God and so we encourage the small groups to give time to this first. We also see that teaching will build people up and we make a small amount of time after worship for this also. But perhaps the single most important element in such groups is to support, encourage and pray for one another. It may be that initially it is difficult for people to express their hopes and goals and their fears and needs in their Christian life, and we don't mind if it takes time. But we are convinced that the housegroup, if it is to be powerful in building people up for the fight, is the place for this.

Leadership in housegroups

For a housegroup to be a safe place in which people can be themselves and grow to maturity takes a particular kind of enabling leadership. Leadership which involves directing the meeting constantly and talking to the group for a majority of the time is unhelpful. Far from being strong, such leadership is, in this context, weak. What is needed is a leader who will set an example in worship and give some brief teaching from the scriptures. Then the leader needs to make time for members of the group to say what they are aiming at in their walk with God and to give time for mutual ministry and prayer. A strong leader is one who is not afraid of listening as people open up. People may be surprised, and in fact say that they have no ambition or goal in their Christian life. In this case, time needs to be given to establishing such a way of thinking, so that we can see that our very purpose as Christians is to grow to be more like Christ. The leader may set Peter's exhortation before the group, to 'make every effort to add to your faith goodness; and to goodness, knowledge; and to knowledge, self-control . . . perseverance . . . godliness . . . brotherly kindness . . . love' (2 Peter 1:5–7). What a goal!

The leader who listens

It is likely that members will already have different godly aspirations and struggles. The leader must make space for these to be expressed. This involves taking a risk: there may well be expression of anger or despair or criticism of the group or (more commonly) the church. Usually behind these is disillusionment and disappointment with oneself.

As a person tells what is on their heart, the leader must not judge, even if he is puzzled by what is being said. His task is to provide a safe atmosphere of love for the mask to be dropped. He needs to respond by saying, 'That sounds very upsetting for you,' or, 'It really seems that God is at work in you at present,' and waiting to hear more. Not every person every week will need to speak. There will not be time. But every one at certain times should be encouraged to open up to the group. If they won't, then it is good for the leader to discuss it in private with the individual. Some will want to monopolise each week with their own problems and again this can abuse the group: a word in private may be needed, or careful leadership in the group.

Gifts and growth

The final priority of such groups in a new church is time for ministry and individual prayer for one another. It may be best for this to occur in smaller groups or all together. Here the gifts of the Spirit are important in revealing needs, bringing healing, imparting more power from the Holy Spirit and building others up. The small group is a place for learning and growing in the use of the gifts and the leaders need to take the risk of saying so, encouraging their use, and being an example themselves. This means risking speaking in a tongue without knowing who will give the interpretation. It means giving a word of knowledge or prophecy perhaps for the first time. This is most likely as frightening as the first time you prayed out loud. But it gets easier, and if we don't begin and step out in faith then our gift will never mature. In this area of mutual ministry, the gifts of the Spirit are given to strengthen and comfort and build up the church. In this area above all, the leader must lead by example.

As a housegroup experiences the power of such mutual support, it is important to take steps to prevent repetition and to set further goals for growth. One way of doing this without embarking on too much teaching is to spend each week applying the Sunday morning sermon. To have five or six open questions about the Sunday teaching (or just one question) and to say where we are at in this area of Christian life can be as helpful as anything in preventing people going round in circles and in encouraging mutual accountability and mutual ministry.

Training leaders

Much of the leadership in housegroups is caught, not taught. As the church planter leads his team, they should pick up, for example, the priority of worship and how to lead it. They will be trained by observing other leaders in action. The church planter will do well to set a goal of identifying and releasing others. However, it is worth noting that this task of leading housegroups is one of the most difficult in the whole church and it should not be assumed that everyone will be able to do it. Other training that is helpful is to gather a group of future leaders together to teach these goals for housegroups. Courses may be needed on subjects such as: the purpose of housegroups; worship in housegroups; building each other up; encouraging spiritual gifts; group dynamics; teaching in housegroups. Time spent on this is important.

Looking out

The danger of the kind of mutual ministry described is that the housegroup becomes inward looking. But the motive for praying for the saints is to equip them to minister in the world. The point of prayer for each other is to impart power. This is the example of Acts 4. The prayer that occurred was in a small group and it was a prayer for power for the church. As the prayer was answered the result was an outward focus: the place was shaken, they began to speak the word of God boldly, and the great missionary activity of the church began.

The housegroup should always retain this outward focus. One way to do this is for each group to aim to divide into two groups and eventually to form a new church in the area where they meet. It is good for two or three housegroups to form the basis of the new church. Build this evangelistic church planting goal into the housegroups from the start. Another practical way of ensuring an outward focus is to insist on the group having one evening in four where they are either involved in evangelism, or planning for it. If this is to be the structure, it is good to go with it from the outset: once groups are established and running, you may find it difficult for group members to 'own' such a threatening idea!

Unity with other churches

What the newly planted local church experiences of the joy of unity among its own members, it should also look for with other churches. The new churches need to see that what Jesus prayed for in John 17 has also to be applied to love between churches. One of the great benefits of being planted out by a mother church is to have that church often praying more for the new church than for itself. The new church also is full of love for the core church and this can be extended to love for other churches in the area. I have a deep respect for Cranham Baptist Church which meets in the same street as the Community Church. We may be placed in the same street, but there is room for both of us and more. There are still 12,000 people in our small area who don't go to any of the four or five churches. I encourage our members to love, respect and pray for the other churches and to seek their well-being and growth above our own. Jesus prayed that we might be one as he and the Father are one, that the world might believe. Jesus and the Father were absolutely one in the purpose of winning the world. No one came to him, Jesus said, unless the Father drew him. Yet it is the Son who 'gives life', They complete each other's work but never compete. Believers within a local church do the same, but so should different local churches complete and complement one another's work, absolutely united in the common goal of winning their community for Christ. This intimacy also is something for which the world still waits.

But how should this witness be carried out? We now move on to examine the third major priority of many of these new churches, namely their intimate involvement with their community as they evangelise.

10

Another kind of famine

This way for the sorrowful city. This way for eternal suffering. This way to join the lost people . . . Abandon all hope, you who enter . . .

Dante

The New Testament teaches that people without God are destined for what Dante called 'the inferno'. But despite this, it is significant that in the entire teaching of the New Testament epistles you will search in vain for any sustained exhortation to evangelise. By contrast, in many of our churches today we are being inundated with books, courses and initiatives on evangelism. Commenting on this recently, evangelist Eric Delve asked: 'Who ever heard of a six-week training course to teach girls who have got engaged how to tell their friends?' The fact is you can't stop them. Perhaps in the days of the New Testament church there was such love that witnessing simply flowed. In all that follows, as we look at this third priority for new churches, we need to remember that at root we need to fall in love with Jesus. Then we'll witness naturally to the delight of knowing him. Having said this, I am not against courses teaching how to tell the gospel to others. I have been involved in many such courses and found them useful. However, there is still no substitute for falling in love!

Another cause for concern is that our whole model for evangelism is at fault as the following story illustrates:

> A group of Canadians were on a weekend bear hunting trip and they had a newcomer in their group. He was a bit proud and pushy and disturbed the group when he challenged them: 'Have any of you ever caught a bear with your bare hands?' They replied that no, they preferred to use their rifles. On arrival at the log cabin he insisted: 'Well, I'm going off to catch a bear with my bare hands: who's coming with me?' They told him bluntly to go if he must but that they preferred more contemporary methods and would stay in the cabin preparing their equipment. Off went the man into the woods only to return screaming for help with a huge grizzly gaining on him with every stride. 'OPEN THE DOOR!' he screamed. As he reached the cabin, the door swung open just in time. He deftly stepped to one side, the bear tore into the cabin. The man slammed the door on him and shouted to his companions: 'You skin that one, I'll go catch another one!'

The evangelist Leighton Ford, who told me this story some years ago, used it to illustrate the fear of many churches of the evangelist coming in and bringing all kinds of disturbing, unsavoury characters into the church. Many people think of mission, if not in such dramatically dangerous terms, with a similar structural model of the evangelist bringing the people into a building, the church. In this case not to be skinned, but to be saved. This is extremely unhelpful as a model. It is seeing the church-as-a-field and not the church-as-a-force. These two models were suggested some years ago by Jerry Cook.[1]

Church-as-a-field

In the church-as-a-field, the church is seen as a building into which people are brought. Even if you are hiring a building exactly the same mentality can obtain. The field is a place where the farmer comes to work; he plants and fertilises and waters and weeds and reaps. Similarly the church-as-a-field is a place or community where members do their work: sidesman, singer, speaker, sweeper, seller of books and tapes, healer, helper, humper of chairs. The believer can be misled about the nature of service, and because these roles are very limited, he can easily become a spectator. This will lead to disaffection and doubt or it will lead to ineffectiveness. When a new church begins, there is very little to do in the church-as-a-field. People who were housegroup leaders may no longer have a group to lead. If the building is rented, there is little opportunity for practical work except for some fevered activity on Sunday. Frustration can easily occur unless members radically change their thinking to view the church-as-a-force.

Church-as-a-force

In this model, **the world is the field and church members are, as individuals, part of a task force which invades society**. We have the goal of becoming Spirit filled believers who can meet the needs of others in society. In this model, the focus is not on our work in the church but our work in the world and how to be more forceful in it. This view of our purpose prevents frustration at loss of 'role within the church' and encourages a fresh commitment to evangelism as a way of life. Once we have this model, we will not worry too much whether what we're into is presence, power, proclamation or whatever kind of evangelism. We'll just get on with making friends with people.

In my view, by far the best evangelism simply involves the church members living in the community, spread thinly as salt is spread through food, giving flavour to the whole. It involves their witness through both works and words, without any programme. The church planting team members need to catch the excitement of this. Sometimes the members of a church planting team have to learn afresh things forgotten because of their wrong understanding of the church-as-a-field. Often, the people most committed to the use of charismatic gifts are those most inept in evangelism. What has happened is that on conversion they have had a host of non-Christian friends. After a year, several relationships have been formed with Christians thus breaking the links with some former friends. After five years, they may be housegroup leaders and very busy with their Christian responsibilities. Very few of their non-Christian friends have remained in touch. After ten years, they may well have reached the zenith of maturity when they know no non-Christian friends at all! This, though a caricature, is a true tragedy for many people in the church. The church planting team is likely to be no exception and radical action needs to be taken if the new church is to survive. I suggest the following steps for all Christians, but particularly for the church planting team.

Steps back to friendship with neighbours

1. **Recognise** that making friends with non-Christians is a top priority.

2. **Repent**, ie change your thinking about what is a valuable use of time. Schedule in days when non-Christians will be asked for a meal or some other friendship-building activity.

3. **Slow down** in your mad rush from chore to chore and talk to those in the shop or office, on the platform or pavement, whom previously you would only have nodded at. Get as interested in others as God is: find out where they're at. Help if possible when need arises.

4. **Say something about Jesus sometime!** The apostle Peter told his friends: always be prepared to make a defence for the hope that is in you. Make the most of every opportunity. Often we have opportunity but are too shy to speak. I have found two things constantly helpful in this. The first is the question: 'Are you a believer?' I seldom find anyone who will answer this question monosyllabically! And it usually leads to the second thing which is to give some testimony.

This may be to talk about your conversion: 'I used to feel similarly, but had an experience which changed my life . . .' Or it may be testimony relevant to the present conversation.

5. Be sensitive to sadness. I remember once talking with a woman who replied to my first question, 'No, I find it hard to believe.' Because she seemed troubled, I then asked if something had happened in her life that had caused this. She then told me of a child she had had who had been still-born. In this case we have a choice: whether to apologise and change the subject, or to share the healing of Jesus. We British prefer the former, but must choose the latter. The testimony that was appropriate here was not about my conversion but to tell briefly of my own son who died in a cot death. I listened at length to her story, then I talked for a moment about the unshakeable fact of the resurrection, about the city where God will wipe away every tear. As the woman was weeping, I asked if she cried often about this. Her reply was that she never cried and moreover had never talked about it since it had happened all those years ago. Behind so many faces which are so seemingly self-assured there lies tragedy as yet untouched by Christ's love and we, the church-as-a-force, have the costly privilege of being Christ's channels.

6. Savour the fruit. Of course, we don't have to have experienced the suffering in question to bring comfort. You don't have to have taken drugs to help an addict. But many Christians have in fact been through the fire. They have known divorce, bereavement, redundancy, accident, a broken home, abortion, illness, rejection, depression, uncertainty at certain points of their lives, perhaps before, perhaps since, conversion. Jesus said: 'Unless an ear of wheat falls to the ground and dies, it remains only a single seed. But if it dies, it produces may seeds.' What God wants to do is take these little deaths in our lives and turn them into fruitfulness. We have often a choice: self pity or spiritual power through suffering. Following the conversation recorded above, this bereaved mother soon committed her life to Christ, was followed by her husband, and shortly afterwards both her parents came to the Lord.

How to sow seed

It may well take time for the church planting team to see fruit of this kind. For several months after seed is sown, nothing can be seen to show that there will be a harvest. We must make sure we don't keep on disturbing the seed's growth by constantly going back to the same people and badgering them. Rather we should toss the seed further afield and generously. The sowing of the seed of the gospel does not happen just with a look, any more than the sowing of barley occurs by the farmer going out and smiling at his field. He has to get the barley, go out at the right time and sow it. So we need to get the word of God, go out with it at the right time and leave it with people. This involves knowing the Bible and being prepared to use the opportunities that come our way. I often ask questions and am interested in the answer. I may ask any of the following:

What do you think of God?
Do you go to church?
What do you think happens when we die?
Are you satisfied with your life at present?
Do you think you are pleasing God at present?
What do you think of the church?
Did you use to go to church?
What do you think is the answer to these problems? (Referring to whatever we have been discussing: hooliganism; child abuse; industrial unrest; pollution – whatever has been in the news . . .)

These may be preceded by some positive statement such as: 'I am very involved in my church. What do you think of the church?' Or: 'My relationship with God is very important to me. What do you think of God?' They also need to be followed by a drawing out of the conversation. If some deep need emerges, as if often will, then offer sympathy and perhaps prayer : don't immediately change the subject! In these ways we can sow seed every day. Surely some of it will bear fruit. The problem is that we sow so little. Or if we do sow it, we sow it in vast, sudden blocks – before a mission, for example – which may appear so artificial to those on the receiving end. The church planting team needs to sow seed as a way of life.

How to penetrate society

The church planting team often has an obvious opportunity to get involved with secular organisations in that it will often meet in a secular building. When we began to consider planting a church in our local community centre, we began a strategy that involved us taking part in as many secular organisations meeting in the centre as possible. I was involved in the committee deciding on policy for the use of the building; others took part in art classes; dance; the coffee bar; the open youth work (which we sent leaders to rather then starting our own); the drama club. Initially, church members were viewed by many with suspicion because of breakdowns in relationships (rows over brownies and guides, etc.) in the past. But now, after three years, they are accepted and respected and relied upon.

Most of the new churches will have a desire to be involved in their community. It is also vital to be involved in political and educational structures, lobbying and working for justice. One of our elders for example, is active as a governor of two schools; another recently was elected a JP; another works for his local Rotary Club; another elder has just joined the now almost completely secular scout group. We have a social concerns pressure group within the church that brings to our attention matters for action. This action may take the form of letters and visits to MPs, ministers or newspapers, or it may involve going to meetings and speaking. It may involve getting our hands dirty and serving.

On the side of the poor

In some areas – such as the one I live in – it is hard to find many who are materially poor. But we have consciously searched for the poor in spirit, and found them in many different situations. First, we had the idea one autumn of writing to all those who had been bereaved in the past three years and had had contact with the church. We invited them to a service on Remembrance Sunday evening at which their loved one would be mentioned by name. I had never seen the church so effortlessly packed. Realising we were meeting a real need in our ageing area, we have embarked on a 'Living with loss' training programme to equip several of our church for long term bereavement counselling.

Similarly, one of our members who had some experience with social services is in the process of opening a Day Care Centre for the housebound. This has a twin aim of befriending and loving those who are confined to their home all day every day. Secondly, they hope to provide a desperately needed break for those who look after them. Thirdly the hope is that some will find Christ. When seeking to evangelise and follow Christ we need to ask: Where is Christ to be found? The answer is clearly : With the poor. In these and many other ways, new and new at heart churches can seek to love the poor in spirit.

Hidden hunger

John Clarke (one of our worship leaders) and Philip Glassborow wrote *Another kind of famine* – a 'song for the lost' which shows another beautifully where all this talk of evangelism should lead us . . .

> There's another kind of famine,
> You don't see it in their eyes,
> You don't see the people dying,
> You don't hear the children cry.
> But they need to hear the message
> That turns darkness into light

And they need to meet with Jesus,
Who says 'I'm the Bread of Life'.

Are you talking to your Father?
Do you share your deep concerns?
Or are you singing 'Hallelujah'
While the man beside you burns?
Do you quench the Holy Spirit?
Don't you feel the need to pray?
Are you feeding on the word of God
At the start of every day?

Send your manna, Lord,
Here in the desert.
Your living water in this barren land.
Give us the words to say . . .
Give us the love to share.
There's another kind of famine,
But the Lord can lead his people by the hand.[2]

If my people . . .

Behind all these initiatives, the new church needs to pray. We are only just realising that this is the first calling from which all else must flow. But we also discover that, far from being a burden, prayer is a refreshment and a joy. Sometimes we have emerged after a four hour session praying for revival to gulp down the night air with such joy and satisfaction as can only come when we know we have been with God. There is a growing desire in the churches for holiness, and that holiness will be marked by prayer. The much loved and still sorely missed David Watson caught this straight from the Holy Spirit when he wrote in his last news letter:

> At about one am on Advent Sunday morning, I had a bad asthmatic attack. In my helplessness, I cried out to God to speak to me. I'm not very good at listening to God, but between one and three am God spoke to me so powerfully and painfully that I have never felt so broken

> before him (and still do).
>
> He showed me that all my preaching, writing and other ministry was absolutely *nothing* compared to my love-relationship with him. In fact, my sheer busyness had squeezed out the close intimacy I had known with him during the first few months of the year after my operation.[3]

I thank God for David's gift for expressing so clearly what is evidently on the Father's heart for us. All else will flow from this. As was said at the start of this chapter, we need to fall in love with Christ and seek his face.

Kingdom evangelism

The excitement of prayer was illustrated unforgettably to me one Saturday morning when a small team met at our Community Church to pray prior to some door to door evangelism. One member was reminded in prayer of Lydia in Acts 16 who was just ready for the gospel when Paul arrived at Philippi. He prayed confidently that the team would be led to people like Lydia whose hearts God had already prepared. After the team had gone off, I decided to visit a needy church member first and only had time to knock on one door before the agreed time to report back. The door was opened by an elderly couple. They talked of their need for God and for healing and after talking about Christ, it seemed right to ask if they would like prayer straight away. They agreed. (In such door to door visiting programmes it certainly seems right to be open to talk, to lead people to Christ or to pray for healing. We need to be sensitive to what seems appropriate.) This couple certainly appeared to be full of faith, which was encouraging as it was the first home that I visited. When I asked what her name was, I should not have been surprised when she replied clearly: 'My name is Lydia.'

Praying or playing?

The postscript to this chapter comes from Leonard Ravenhill and you can hear the passion coming through as he waxes lyrical in this highly quotable (or unquotable, depending on your tastes) purple passage:

> No man is greater than his prayer life. The pastor who is not praying is playing; the people who are not praying are straying. Poverty-stricken as the Church is today in many things, she is most stricken here, in the place of prayer. We have many organizers, but few agonizers; many players and payers, few pray-ers; many singers, few clingers; lots of pastors, few wrestlers; many fears, few tears; much fashion, little passion; many interferers, few intercessors; many writers, but few fighters. Failing here, we fail everywhere.[4]

For years, I have kept this haunting expression of the need to pray close by me. Church planters need to begin, continue and finish always in prayer.

11

'As each part does its work . . .'

What matters in the Church is not religion but the form of Christ, and its taking form amidst a band of men.

Dietrich Bonhoeffer

The fourth clearly identifiable priority in so many of the new churches is the idea of sending out evangelistic or faith-sharing teams. Many established churches see the need for this too. Again, it is clearly something the Holy Spirit is doing today.

There is a legend which tells how Jesus went back to heaven after his time here on earth. Even in heaven he bore the marks of the cross. The angels were talking and Gabriel said:

'Master, you must have suffered terribly for man down there.'

'I did,' said Jesus.

'And', said Gabriel, 'do they all know how you loved them and what you did for them?'

'Oh no. Not yet. Just a few people in Palestine know.'

'What have you done to let everyone know about it?' Jesus was asked.

'I have asked Peter, James and John and a few others

to make it their business to tell others about me, and others others. Until the farthest man on the widest circle knows about what I have done.'

Gabriel looked doubtful – for he knew men. 'Yes, but what if they get tired? What if others forget. What if in the future people just don't tell others?'

And Jesus answered: 'I haven't made any other plans. I'm counting on them . . .'

Whoever thought up this ancient story (re-told by, among others, William Barclay) understood a vital principle of Jesus' ministry: that of training and sending out teams. Jesus had a masterplan to win the world and he manoeuvred singlemindedly to his goal. His great work was to preach and bring the good news of the kingdom. His great secret was to lay aside his life at Calvary to break the powers and to cancel sin. But his great strategy for the future was to **select** people, **share his life** with them, **train** them in the work of the kingdom, **send them** out in teams, **supervise** what they did and then to **hand over** the work to them. As R E Coleman has so helpfully shown,[1] his emphasis was not on the big crowds, although he did speak to thousands on several occasions. Rather, he gave himself to the few, the twelve or the three. And the nearer he got to the end of his life, the more time he spent with the few. Even before they were ready, he sent them out in pairs to heal the sick, cast out demons and even raise the dead. They went off in teams with Christ's news almost as soon as they had decided to become his followers.

Today, one of the hallmarks of the new churches is this training and 'teaming it'. 'Leadership, spelt TEAM' is how John Noble aptly puts it in a chapter title in his book *House Churches* (Kingsway, 1988). He goes on to say this:

> If we reject the biblical, Christ-ordained concept of team, Jesus will raise up others who will practise it. Already Christian leaders from all sorts of backgrounds are recognising the soundness of building teams. Increasing numbers of churches are reconstituting their leadership away

from the one-man pastor served by deacons (or in some cases ruled by deacons) to an eldership team plus deacons. Also, numbers of strong local churches are developing teams which they can release to assist groups who are less gifted and endowed than themselves, both at home and overseas. And, what's more, these teams are sympathetic and helpful towards one another. They are waking up to the fact that Europe is now the neediest continent on earth and there is more than enough room for all who are called to work in this harvest field. Thank God for what we have, but the best is yet to come!

Travelling teams

I well remember when I first became a Christian, I was invited to join a Christian theatre group called 'Breadrock' for a two-week street theatre mission. We lived in community and spent the morning worshipping and praying, the afternoon rehearsing and the evening performing and evangelising. It was my first experience of a small group, my first experience of intimate worship, my first experience of evangelism in the open air. I loved every moment of it. I had been working as an actor in a Theatre In Education team and the contrast between the world and the community of Christians was shatteringly marvellous. Since those days under Paul Burbridge and Murray Watts' leadership, I have been thoroughly committed to the idea of Team. When I finished training for the ordained ministry I was amazed to be asked to be a curate who was not going to work so much in one parish as to lead a faith-sharing team. The Cranham Park Fellowship has had such a ministry (the 'Together Team') for around fifteen years, and a new leader was needed. I came and began to build a new team. I chose some new, some experienced, some old, some young Christians. We travelled around Essex and further afield leading weeks of mission or weekends for renewal and training. Always, the Holy Spirit came. I can't remember a trip where no one was converted. To begin with, we worked with an arts presentation of songs and sketches and dance. But more recently, we have moved to an emphasis on renewing, equipping and healing. This going out with the gospel strengthens those who are receiving and those who are giving.

It is good for a church to come aside for a special period to consider the call of God as this letter suggests:

Dear friends,

I really want to thank all of our new friends at Cranham for the joy you, with the help of our Lord, have instilled into our family. I was so opposed to this mission and now I am just so thankful for it. I really believed that a mission like this was not the right way at all to make God's church come alive; how wrong I was. I went to a prayer meeting for the first time on Tuesday and actually prayed out loud with a great crowd of people around me. I just kept hearing this prayer in my head over and over again and I'd actually spoken a few words before I even realised that I was talking. It was a great relief to actually share it with so many people. I can't describe this inner joy and peace that I feel, but I'm sure you have all felt it too.

With love, Tina.

The joy of conversion or the fulness of the Spirit may well be experienced in the receiving church. But in the sending church, a similar joy will abound as people return with stories of God at work. Jesus knew such a joy when his teams returned that he could not contain his praise to his Father in heaven (Luke 10:21).

Getting a team going

Getting the church regularly to send away some of its strongest members is a calling which needs a response of faith and action. But the first requirement is the call. This can, like any other call, be subject to fleshly ambition. It is possible to want to start sending out teams with the gospel because it is 'the thing to do'. Leaders need to discuss carefully whether this is something that is really from God. Often, a church needs to wait, and in its babyhood it may well need all its energy just to feed and grow strong. But there may come a time sooner than you think when God says, 'GO!' It seems that what is important then is to set apart a leader (preferably full-time) who will take the step of faith of saying, 'I feel called to go,' even before he has been invited to go anywhere!

This involves the leadership in a certain amount of risky living which is generally good and wholesome, provoking the leaders to seek for God to open some doors. I remember feeling this vulnerability when appointed to lead a faith-sharing team in the Chelmsford diocese: what if no one wanted us to come? We asked advice and tested the calling, but in the end we had to take a step of faith and say Yes without knowing how things would work out, but knowing God had called us. This is true particularly of travelling ministries such as that of evangelist. He will do well to be supported by and based in a local church but there will come a point at which he has to say, 'Yes, this is my calling,' and probably say so publicly.

Once a leader is appointed

Forming such a team needs careful planning and training in the early stages. When we began the ministry the team spent hours together in training and worship and in getting to know one another. And this is vital when beginning such a work. Apart from worshipping and seeking God together, I felt it was of importance to train members in how to lead someone to Christ and how to pray for someone to be filled with the Spirit. More recently, we have trained on the healing ministry and the other gifts of the Holy Spirit. This initial preparation involved meeting once a week for a year. Now, however, after several years together, there are many people with whom we work easily and little specific preparation is needed as we are already in relationship. We don't need so much to prepare together for the meetings as to prepare our hearts before God. Indeed we went off recently for a two-week trip to Africa with only one preparation meeting preceding.

Where to go?

The best place to start is at home, which is where, as the old proverb says, charity begins. You may well want to respond to the needs of your own community and do some door to door work as a team over a period of weeks. This can direct the group to the Lord in prayer as nothing else, and cause the regular exercise of the faith muscles, which is so good for the Christian. In addition, opportunities usually exist locally in hospitals, old people's centres, prisons, schools and shopping centres for the presentation of the good news. So the team can and will do well to begin some mobile mercy ministry of this kind right where you are.

Then it may be that as people hear of your work, invitations from further afield will come. Or it may be you will make your work known through friendship networks; you may publish a leaflet describing your ministry; you may wish to use some mailing of other church leaders to inform them of your desire to give away what you have received. Any or all of these are good provided one's motive is mercy and love: the desire to bring the kingdom of God to those who are struggling or lost.

Counting the cost

As with sending out a church planting team, there is a cost. This can be in terms of certain people in the church no longer appearing at all the meetings! The team will find it has a focus that is often outside the local church and there can be conflicts of interest that need to be worked out. But in all these things, provided the initiative to go out has come from God, and agreement has been reached among the church leadership that this is a calling from God, then we can stop minding losing several of our strongest members from other local pastoral responsibilities. And we will find again and again that if we give away it will be given back to us in terms of confidence in God and joy and broader vision as teams return.

Healing ministry teams

Much of what has been said about travelling teams will apply to the setting apart of people to minister healing in church meetings week by week. Leadership and organisation is important as is training and exercising faith. Since the visits of John Wimber to Britain, the confidence of the church that God is a God of power and authority over sickness, both mental and physical, has grown by a kind of quantum leap. Many have come into a completely new experience of what it means to have the Holy Spirit come upon them 'as he had come on [the disciples] at the beginning' (Acts 11:15). This has brought a sudden but lasting confidence that God in his mercy wants to touch many in and outside the churches in a physical as well as intellectual way with his love and with his healing.

Equipping

Sometimes people can feel excluded from such ministry for a variety of reasons. Perhaps past pain or failure has led to a loss of expectation. But in fact, part of our equipping for such work comes when past disappointments are healed by a present appointment with the God of glory.

My own experience was that in 1982 we lost our first son in a cot death. For several months afterwards I felt physically sick when any glib (as I thought) reference was made to the healing power of God. I had prayed for healing as I held my boy in my arms but no answer had come. It was a period of agony followed by drab colourless attempts to pick up the pieces of ministry; then came a renewal of strength and some healing from God, especially through a knowledge of the fact of the resurrection. But when people asked our team to come and teach on healing, my answer was always No. Evangelism, being filled with the Spirit, worship, prayer . . . Yes, but not healing.

Then in 1985 came a day I'll never forget. I'd gone to help lead worship and to hear David Pytches speak locally at a training day. During the mid-morning coffee break, David strolled over to me and placed his hand on my heart and prayed that God would send his Spirit on me. What I can only describe as a physical weight seemed to press me to my seat and then on to my back: something I had never known before. I was laughing and then crying at the same time. One of David's team came over and prayed with me for a deep work of cleansing and healing. A considerable time later, when I sat up, I knew that everything was different. I had a new confidence in the power of God. I did not understand why my son had died. But I knew that God was mighty and powerful and awesome and . . . apparently . . . interested in me! From that day to this, I have prayed for the sick and distressed with a completely new confidence.

I have told this story at some length because it illustrates one person's equipping for doing the works of the kingdom. When the new church wants to set apart a team for this work, the important thing is that people are equipped for ministry. This may happen in different ways: there may be a word from God in prayer that comes with conviction to the heart, and that may be all. There may however be physical signs when seeking God about this: heat in the hands, or tingling, or trembling or shaking or weeping or falling. These are manifestations that can be seen, reminding us of the signs of the Holy Spirit that could be seen in Acts 8. On that occasion, Simon was so impressed by what he saw that he offered money to buy this ability. We today should open our eyes to look at those in the congregation anointed by God for this ministry.

Others may know their calling to this ministry because of the burden they feel in their heart when they pray. As in all areas of Christian life, most of the above signs can be counterfeit or true. What is needed is to check the consistency of character and Christian discipline and the fruit in the lives of those applying to join the church's healing ministry teams.

Training and releasing

Alongside the anointing should go some teaching over a period of months and some local ordering of the ministry. Much has been written about how to do this and one of the best guides is David Pytches' guidelines in *Come Holy Spirit*. After some teaching, it is good to pray that God would set apart some individuals for regular ministry. It is then good publicly to commission them and to publish some kind of statement of who they are and why they have been appointed. The congregation needs to have confidence in those to whom they are coming for prayer.

In a new church, it is quite possible that the initial ministry team will be formed from the church planting team, which is ideal as they will already be in relationship. Our way of working is this: we do not operate with set teams but small groups of two to three will normally assemble each time to pray for each person coming forward. At least one experienced person should be there and this one will lead and seek to include the others, to any of whom may be given special revelation or gifting for the ministry in hand. The purpose of such ministry is not long-term counselling, but to invoke the Holy Spirit 'to bring salvation, wholeness, healing, deliverance and peace to broken people, relationships, and situations – between God and man, between man and man – and in the personality of the individual'.[2]

In this, we need each other. We need the aspect of teamwork that we find in the New Testament. A foundation principle of many of these new churches is that they will want to see members equipped, trained and released to bring the kingdom of God, the rule of God, the healing and deliverance of God to all those who need it.

Teams of elders and deacons

John Noble is right about churches from different backgrounds choosing to be led through a group of elders. In our situation, we have *appointed* a team of elders, whereas we *select* a church council (which in my view corresponds to a team of deacons). It is a common practice in the church to have two groups which overlap and yet which are distinct, one of which may be appointed and the other which is elected. Broadly speaking, the task of one is pastoral and the task of the other is administrative.

The role of the elders falls into three categories: firstly to direct the affairs of the church. We see this in Paul's writing to Timothy. Here the elders are going to be those who are leading the church and among those showing where the church should be going. In conjunction with the full-time staff they will be seeking direction from God as to the particular areas in which he would have us work. They will not, therefore, be acting as a brake on the work of God but rather spurring it forward in all wisdom and humility under God. The second area in which they will work will be a pastoral one; we see this in the experience of Moses where the elders were appointed in order to judge between people and help people reach agreement, and therefore growth, in their spiritual life. The third area of work for the elders is that of mutual support and accountability for leaders, particularly the vicar or pastor and full-time members of staff.

It is clearly a biblical principle that leadership should be plural and that leaders should have the security of being able to share decisions and the decision making process with others. In the counsel of many, wise decisions can be made. So their work will be in terms of setting goals together, pastoring the church together and advising the leadership as regards various courses of action. In all these things they will need to be men and women of prayer. The pattern set in Acts 6 of there being those in the church who are able to devote themselves to prayer and the word should be one held dear by the elders.

Commenting briefly from an Anglican point of view, the elders have no legal role within the Church of England and it is the church council (PCC) which has the responsibility for the financial affairs and the direction of the church, along with the bishop. But it is a wise PCC that will recognise the need for a group of godly advisers to help them ascertain what God is saying to the church. In practice, in our situation, the two groups overlap with at least one elder from each congregation also serving on the PCC.

Ideally, the eldership should be an example to the whole church of what it means to be a team. But how do we know who to appoint and when to appoint them? When we started Cranham Community Church, I was keen to appoint elders immediately, but was checked by advice from Campbell McAlpine. He strongly counselled patience. The idea of waiting and watching and seeing who was functioning already in an eldership role in all but name sounded wise to me. So I watched to see who it was that people were turning to for advice and who had a vision for the future of the church. I felt that relationship is vital: there is no point forcing yourself to spend hours in discussion, re-creation, intercession and planning with those you find really difficult to relate to. There is real wisdom in choosing people you can get on with like a house on fire, ie where one idea ignites another and then another until the prayer is roaring up to heaven like smoke!

It was not until at least a year after beginning to meet that our first two elders were appointed. They were men of whom all the above was true. This is not to say that we agreed on everything: far from it. But our friendship was such that any such disagreement could be driving us on to seek God, rather than depressing and dampening our fire . . . at least most of the time! The same was true of these men's wives: there was and is absolute unity of vision with them, as well as great fun and friendship too. Campbell sometimes says that a wife can disqualify her husband from eldership, and I would add that so can a husband disqualify his wife. The New Testament is clear about the requirements for eldership: godly personal life and character, order in relationships in the home, and a good reputation in the community. We should check this too when considering appointing.

Finally, it is good if the team have complementary gifts. Ephesians 4 tells us God appoints apostles, prophets, evangelists, pastors and teachers so that the church might be strengthened. In an eldership team we should seek to combine those with pastoral gifts with the teachers and prophets. We have recently added someone with particular evangelistic gifts to our team because of this perceived lack. Having said this, it is important not to hurry and do this if you are not sure you have the right person. It is better to start with only two elders who are right than a large group we're not sure of. I have waited nearly two years before being free to make the above appointment.

In an ideal world, the deacons or church council will also function as team. In a new church, you have the opportunity to lay some new foundations and to get away from the image of boring, stuffy, conservative, deathly meetings with the vicar or minister impatiently trying to 'get something through the PCC' – rather than in the way one might try to 'get through the Dartford tunnel' in the rushhour, if you live near us – hopelessly!

In my view the PCC, diaconate, or 'board' or whatever, should correspond to what we read of in Acts 6:1 and 2. Here the church leaders were concerned not to neglect the word of God because of the 'daily ministration' (*diakonia*) of serving (*diakoneō*) at tables. The apostle Paul describes the appointment of deacons in 1 Timothy 3:8–13. From this we assume that it is good that some should particularly be involved in organising our service to the community. This should be the role of the council and hence, some years ago, we changed their subgroup names from 'PCC subcommittee' to 'PCC workgroup', reflecting the understanding that the deacons are there to **do the work** (and get others to do the work) of ministry. They should therefore be people of action and not just of words. Perhaps an even more accurate name would be 'PCC ministry team'. Deacons are teaming up to reach a lost world and thinking and praying about strategy and finance required and giving oneself and one's goods to the task in hand. Thus **team** thinking needs to invade every part of the new churches' life, with no exceptions.

12

Troubleshooting

Between the idea
And the reality
between the motion
And the act
Falls the Shadow.

T S Eliot

A church planting team will encounter trouble as it tries to bring the plant to maturity. Whether it is culture, birth pains, questions of independence, finances, premises or spiritual attack, we need to be as prepared as possible.

Trouble with the soil

To return to the gardening analogy, some plants will flourish in soil where others will die. In suburbia one kind of church may be appropriate. But in inner-city Liverpool, another kind may be appropriate. Strictly speaking this is not trouble with the soil, but trouble with the plant. We need to choose an appropriate type of plant. In a youth culture for example, a completely different kind of church may be needed, as has recently happened in a church planting development in Sheffield. This is the famous (or infamous!) '9 o'clock service' at St Thomas Crooke's. Here a completely different model of (extremely loud) worship, using simultaneous screen projection, informality and simple direct preaching and an expectation of signs and wonders, has succeeded in growing a congregation of 400 from the punk and street and student culture in a space of two years.

If your soil is proving unproductive, identify what kind of soil you are trying to plant in and choose a plant that suits it. Radical change may need to be made in the middle-class expectations surrounding church life. Lack of space prevents further analysis of what should be done. But Monica Hill has some helpful comments on the different demands of the rural, inner-city, immigrant, Muslim, Asian and African communities.[1] All these have different requirements.

It cannot be stressed too strongly that trouble may come from not properly matching the type of plant to the soil with which you are working. Robert Scott-Cook (quoted by Monica Hill) has detailed his experience of church planting on large housing estates. Anyone aiming to plant a church in such an environment would do well to take careful account of his seven basic principles for such work. They are: understand the environment; identify with the community (ie live, shop, be educated and participate there); reach your neighbours; build a family atmosphere; help whole families; nurture young converts and train leadership; and, finally, continuity of care. Failure to match type of church to type of community may result in such trouble that the baby fails even to come to birth.

Trouble at birth

Churches are planted for a variety of different reasons. Some years ago Michael Griffiths coined some memorable terms to describe the different processes: First, there is **spontaneous schismatic outstep**: this is a split in a church which results eventually in a breakaway group meeting somewhere nearby. Often the motive is not to plant a church. Rather a conflict of personality or theology has occurred which cannot be resolved. First one or two leave, then others follow. It is very rare that a planned strategy occurs. The group is hurt and sometimes distressed but may well be partly in the right. They may well be frustrated with the lack of vision and stick-in-the-mud nature of local leadership. The old wineskin is unable to contain the new wine of the Spirit and it bursts out. The people eventually gather together in a home or rented building and begin to worship together. For such a group, this period is one of great crisis and the survival and future health of the premature baby will depend largely on the calibre and spirit of the leadership. Are they men and women who have become bitter and judgmental or are they genuine, open to God and keeping no record of wrongs? Are there leaders who can lead and feed the group in the way described in the previous chapters? I have known such groups founder and disappear and I have known others grow into churches of great power and effectiveness.

One such was in Washington DC. There was no plan to leave the mother church, but individuals were asked to leave. One of those asked to leave was on the staff. He worked out his notice with sorrow but without bitterness, and always praying for a change of heart. After several weeks a group of leaders among those who had left wrote a careful letter to invite this man to lead them. Such was the godly, submissive spirit of the letter that the offer was accepted. So began a church ejected prematurely from its mother but given a healthy start by the leaders' forgiving bitterfree spirit. So apart from the soil, the first trouble might be at birth. Hard, hurt, unloving attitudes will kill a church sooner or later: get rid of them!

Another kind of birth is the **spontaneous schismatic inpush**. Here another group targets an area and 'parachutes' a team in to form a new church. For Michael Griffiths, this 'is essentially sectarian, usually with some new doctrinal emphasis behind it, teaching that they are the only true biblical Christians: thus existing Christians and churches are despised, regarded as inferior, unenlightened and, at best, second class Christians'.[1] This may be a bit strong, but certainly there is the danger of wrong attitudes and the work of the devil on both sides. The incoming group are tempted to be proud, to proselytise, seeking to draw people out of existing churches. The established congregation may be provoked to anger, jealousy, fear, slander and gossip: all very unhelpful. This kind of 'parachute' planting should only be undertaken with patience, grace, generosity and consultation. Michael Griffiths faces the fact that most of our present denominations began in this way, with 'Baptists and Brethren considering themselves more biblical and enlightened than the misguided institutional establishment! Recent developments may be seen only as the latest eruption of something that has happened many times before.'

Roger Forster describes his own experience of this type of outreach, a kind of combination of 'inpush' and 'outstep', at the start of the Ichthus movement: 'Before we began our work, I visited other local ministers to inform them of our intentions and received nothing but encouragement to go ahead. The housing areas we were going to concentrate on were not considered fruitful ground and local ministers had enough to do already: so their blessing was readily given . . .'[2] It may be that the rapid growth of the work has been partly due to this untraumatic birth experience.

Denominational outreach is the name given to the third and final group of church planters identified by Michael Griffiths. An existing denominational group develop a daughter congregation on a new or unevangelised housing estate – like the planned growth of the Scottish Baptists, most of whose congregations have a new outreach in an adjacent area. For Griffiths, this natural growth is legitimate, whereas other forms are ' "illegitimate" in that they have no obvious father or mother on the immediate scene and because such growth is often the product of unresolved conflicts, and consequent schism.'[1] For myself, I would hesitate to criticise any group, knowing that there are still so many millions in the nation who do not know Christ, that there is more than enough room for every group. Sometimes breaking away, and breaking new ground, are simply unavoidable if the call of God is upon those involved. But trauma at the birth is the first danger that a church will face and careful cleansing, confession, correction of attitudes to those within and outside the church, are very important if the work is not to go sour.

Cutting the umbilical cord

A few weeks ago I received a distressed phone call from a friend to tell me of a close relative who had just had a child nearly strangled at birth by the umbilical cord. Brain damage was apparently inevitable and, tragically, the child died some hours later. The same threat to the health and growth and very life of the new congregation is there if the relationship with the mother church is not handled as carefully and decisively as the cord should be. As the new church begins, take care to allow its members to make the break with all their responsibilities in the mother church. They may be housegroup leaders, cleaners, evangelists, pastors. A youth leader's mid-week duties may not apparently conflict with the meetings of the new church. But the cord must be cut. It should be cut carefully: sometimes the start of the church needs to be delayed until people can lay down their responsibilities, but not delayed too long. This is particularly true of the leader of the new work. He may seem easily able to do both old and new things: after all the new church is small. But to hold on to him and not let him go is tantamount to the risk of strangling the new church. Cut the cord: it's the only way to be born!

Teething and potty training

In the new church's infancy, extra stress can be present because of smallness. To put it bluntly: in a church of three hundred members, people can go through trauma in relative privacy. In a church of thirty to fifty, everyone knows! For those of a more private disposition this can be an intolerably unsafe invasion of privacy. When a new church starts, people are nervous and do over-react, rather like when a baby is teething. I remember some of my four adored children keeping me and Annie up all night and all of us being in a bad mood the following day: that's just teething! Similar stress can arise from wet beds and worse. It is a help to see that teething trouble is par for the course when you're a small church. One antidote is to decide positively to enjoy the babyhood. Each new event is a joy and a thrill; each new 'first' should be relished rather than resented. The new church learning to talk to her Father may be hesitant, but is a joy. First Christmas; first housegroup changes, first bout of 'flu laying off half the membership . . . first row!; first times of refreshing; first teaching series. All these can and should be recognised as being liable to teething trouble and this should help the group to be encouraged to carry on.

Adolescence and leaving home

One major question that can lead to trouble at home and at church is: when should the child leave home? Some church planting groups have as their goal that the new work should be self-sufficient within a set period of time, perhaps as short as one year. Some have the aim of financial sufficiency and independence and feel that the only way for the new church to reach full potential is by it attaining complete independence. This is the model followed by the Vineyard and by many house churches and Baptist churches

You know you're in church planting when . . .
infants can crawl from the nursery to the pulpit in 19.3 seconds.

in England. One advantage is that the churches become self-supporting. The church learns to have faith in God for other needs as it learns to trust him for financial needs. The International Correspondence Institute has published a step by step manual: *Starting New Churches*. Here the assumption is that a new church needs to work as fast as possible towards independence. Reasons are given such as these: 'Self-supporting churches provide for unlimited growth'; 'Self-government to promote growth of spiritual ministries and respect for its own leaders'. This is a perfectly valid view where a group are called to plant in an area several miles distant from the first.

Where the churches are going to be quite close geographically a different dynamic may operate. In Cranham, we have felt strongly that we need each other. There is also an evangelistic power in unity. Jesus said: 'a city set on a hill cannot be hidden'. So a large church with a common strategy can at times have more clout than several small independent ones. The whole can have a greater effect than the sum of its parts. In addition to this, there is something healthy about whole congregations loving each other and spending money on one another. If one congregation needs £15,000 to build an extension for its children's work, it is good for the whole church to raise it. Office equipment and computing, copying, printing, etc. may all be of a higher standard if centrally organised. We have congregations of between eighty and 250 who meet separately on Sunday mornings. These units are broken down into cells for the purpose of pastoral care and nurture, with the congregational leader having oversight for not more than 150 adults. The congregations then meet together on Sunday nights for a celebration meeting where, we hope, we can consider more of what God is calling us to for our whole church and whole area.

We have been encouraged in this model by the advice and example of Roger Forster and the Ichthus Christian Fellowship in south-east London which has grown so rapidly and planted so many congregations but still remained one church. Roger writes: 'The area church consisting of a number of congregations is not new. The Methodist movement among others practised it; the advantage of the celebration meetings is the inspiration they minister to Christians to know and feel they are part of something bigger than just the 60–70 people at congregational meetings. The supernatural is often released in large-scale gatherings and people experience more of the power and presence of God.'[2]

When a church commissions a team, it is good to know which model is anticipated and to be clear about it. In our case, there was for some an assumption that the goal of independence was the right one. Through a combination of factors – biblical convictions, practical demands, a timely houseparty with Roger Forster – this strategy changed to our present one. But the change brought much heartache for a time and it would have been better both to have been godlier and clearer from the start. Both models (and other variations) are no doubt equally valid, having their advantages and disadvantages. But each church must have the right model for its situation.

The next generation

Stress can result when one leader leaves and another takes on leadership. Where a leader is raised up from within the group, things may be easier, but not necessarily. The vital principle is to choose the one who is already leading. People will not change just because they are given new responsibility. What is needed is to see who the congregation are looking to and who has leadership gifts and vision and to see whether God is giving them a calling to the work.

Where someone comes in from elsewhere, a new generation of church life is starting. This can be a wonderful period of honeymoon and growth; or it can just as often be stressful. If it is the latter, it may be because of the strength of the relationship with the original church planter. Arguably, this relationship with the leader may well be more important to people in a new church than in an established church. When the relationship comes to an end, and a new one starts with a new leader, special love needs to be exercised on both sides. It is, however, a perfectly biblical and therefore workable change. The apostle Paul stayed about two years in Corinth in all 'teaching them the word of God' (Acts 18:11). Then he planted, with the disciples whom he found there, a new work in Ephesus, with its daily discussions in the lecture hall of Tyrannus. He stayed in Ephesus for two to three years before leaving for Macedonia. History does not relate who, if any, among the Ephesian elders took over leadership, but it does state the strength of affection between them and Paul later on as they wept and embraced before accompanying him to his ship (Acts 20:37). A change in leadership can be eased considerably if the congregation's leaders have a strong hand in choosing a successor. Then a choice can be 'owned' by the whole church because its leaders were responsible for it.

When the baby gives birth

I was rocked, recently, by an article in a French newspaper. This particular article told of a nine-year-old girl in South America giving birth to a baby son. 'Is it a record?' the paper wanted to know. Part of our distress comes from feeling, 'Poor thing: she's too young! Let her enjoy her childhood,' and the like. Clearly, the same could be true of a new church: for some time it will be too young to reproduce. But there is no clear answer to the question: When is a church old enough to give birth?

The answer will depend on whether the new church is an independent unit or one of several congregations. The answer may also have to do with size rather than age. If a church is independent and has an active adult membership of 150 plus, it is big enough to plant. Some churches will have been around for years having reached about the 200 mark and never having had a baby. In some cases that's as sad as a woman finding she is barren. But for many reading this, it is still not too late.

When the model is that of an area church consisting of several congregations, two or more congregations will join to give members to the new church. This means the congregations can be smaller. This year our first church plant, with a congregation of a hundred, joined with our original congregation, numbering about 250, to plant our fourth congregation. They gave until it hurt, lovingly, joyfully, willingly, faithfully. The signs are that all those who have left are being replaced this same year by a group currently preparing to come into membership.

Oh no! not pregnant again?

Some of my friends have as many as six children. When the news of another pregnancy breaks on the grandparents, it is not always met with the greatest enthusiasm. They know the strain on the parents and the toll on mum's energy levels. Exactly the same is true in church childbirth. It is an exhausting and exacting process. Our parish church, St Luke's, had two babies under three at one stage and felt very anaemic for a while as a result. Other churches nearly die in childbirth. And yet, it is worth it. What is advisable is to plan things as carefully as possible. Compensate for resultant weakness with rest, good food, recuperation. But always retain the romance of being fruitful and the joy that comes from knowing that, even though there is a cost, churches are made for this!

Finding somewhere to live

The new family will soon need somewhere to live: here lies one great concern, but it can also be a great opportunity. There are three main possibilities with regard to buildings: to buy one; to be lent or rent one with exclusive use; or to hire or borrow one at different times each week.

The first option is obviously the most expensive but is not impossible. At present one of my former colleagues is negotiating to buy a school, at a cost of only £500,000, for a permanent Christian youth and community centre and to plant a new church there on Sundays. In some parts of the country such a venture would be quite impossible because of prohibitive costs, but in others, it is feasible. Flexibility and great imagination are important. The advantages of owning a building can be great in terms of control, but not if it imposes a crippling financial burden.

Avoiding having a mortgage round your neck

The disadvantages of buying buildings were powerfully expressed in Howard Snyder's classic *New Wineskins*, published by Marshall, Morgan and Scott in 1975. Snyder argued particularly against the American pastor-superstar tendency, and on behalf of the poor. With passion, he detailed how 'our church buildings witness to the **immobility; inflexibility; lack of fellowship; pride** and **class div-**

isions in the modern church.' Partly as a reaction against this, many leaders prefer to lease permanently. Whether this is a warehouse or a church, the advantage is the lack of initial capital outlay, although substantial sums can be spent on furnishing.

In our situation, our first church plant took place in a condemned (structurally!) Brethren chapel. In this case, the use of the building was given to us, though its deeds are held by a national Christian charitable trust. We spent an initial £40,000 on underpinning and furnishing the building and have since added a portacabin for children's work. The great advantage of permanent possession is that we can have control over how the building looks. In addition, we can run a playgroup there and an old people's pop-in centre during the daytime. As well as this, we can use the building for prayer late into the night: not possible where a secular building with a caretaker is being hired for short periods.

Another kind of long term leasing often seen in the States is where a warehouse has been rented on a long lease and so semi-permanent alterations can be made, and offices set up to function in the same way as if the church owned the building. Some analysts have commented that, just as people prefer to shop in a supermarket to a corner store today, so there may be benefits from the larger 'supermarket size' church. This is not to suggest it should be like a market place: the Lord of the church has already turned the tables over on any such tendency. It is merely good to be aware that there is a power when many come together to form the 'house of prayer for all nations' that Jesus calls for. Whenever I drive past our local Carpetland, MFI or Toys 'R' Us warehouses, I wonder when one of them will be housing a church. I expect to see a trend of some enterprising groups in this country taking some of these over in the future. Even as I write, I have heard of one group negotiating to buy an aircraft hangar: they can anticipate an early ban on jokes about the worship taking off etc!

Hiring a church

The third major possibility for the new church team is to rent a building at different times of the week. Within this, there are two kinds of hiring. One is simply to hire for three hours on Sundays; the other is to try to gain some permanent accommodation during the week. It will depend on one's needs and goals, but this latter course can have great advantages. For example, our community church, which meets in the community centre, secured a permanent office there for its full-time leader as well as, for a time, an office for his secretary. The community association welcomed the idea of a pastor being available at the heart of the community. I don't take this for granted and am very grateful to them for it. At the present, among other things, he makes himself available there one morning a week for any who want advice or help. This permanent accommodation also extends to a large walk-in cupboard for storing bulky p.a. equipment, banners, bookstall, worship books and projectors. The result is that at the 9.30 am setting up, the workload and 'humping' that is the bane of the church planting team's life, is drastically diminished, to the encouragement of all concerned!

Other advantages of being involved in a secular building for more than just an hour or two per week are manifold. The Christians can act as salt spread thinly through the

You know you're in church planting when . . .
every piece of furniture has to be put away after the service.

whole operation, adding their own particular groups to other ones. For example, we organise jointly with the community association a monthly 'Carers' lunch' for the caring professions, to give support and to make relationships and to be informed about new initiatives. It is not a Christian meeting, but it is a Christian initiative. In turn, the Christians can gain a healthy respect for the dedication of many others who serve in the community but who are not part of the church. They can be challenged in a positive way by this. Too often a whole Christian community retreats from the world and becomes separate and superior instead of serving, daring to be involved, and acting as salt and light.

I don't take the provision we have for Cranham Community Church for granted, particularly as it came after a protracted wait. When searching for a breakthrough in this department, both prayer and action are very important: action in terms of visiting councillors, officials, community leaders and making relationships with them. Very often, such people will do all they can to help, and this is a good opportunity to get to know them and the tensions and conflicts they face. Even a delay can be beneficial in terms of new relationships formed. The importance of prayer to God for an open door and for individuals involved in the decision cannot be overstressed. There may be spiritual opposition, of which more in the next chapter. This delay may also be an opportunity for the team to draw near to God and find satisfaction in him alone. The prophet Habbakuk learnt a lesson (Habbakuk 3:17–18) which would benefit all church planters in the waiting period:

> Though the fig-tree does not bud
>   and there are no grapes on the vines,
> though the olive crop fails
>   and the fields produce no food,
> though there are no sheep in the pen
>   and no cattle in the stalls,
> Yet I will rejoice in the LORD,
>   I will be joyful in God my Saviour.

It is a great gain if the team can learn to find satisfaction in God and in him alone . . . it may even be that God will hold back an answer on some of these questions, as he tests our love for him and our contentment in him alone.

Costs, caretakers and county councils

A second kind of renting is of course the option to move in and out in the space of just a few hours on Sunday. If this is the plan, it is quite often a school that will be hired. Unless it is a church school which may (and should!) let you have the building for nothing, this is likely to be the more expensive option. I'm told that at Ichthus at present, advice has gone out only to use schools as a last resort because of the cost. With the introduction of LMS (which gives to individual schools in England and Wales the responsibility of running their own lettings), it is quite likely such charges will rise. It costs us several hundred pounds each Sunday that we need to use our local school hall. Again, negotiation and prayer are important. In the end, a group have to balance the cost and the advantages and see if they feel they can proceed by faith. Jesus taught, in his analogy about building the tower, about the need for careful planning. But in the end, to proceed by faith in God is always going to be necessary, and there will always be an element of risk to this.

Planning ahead for growth

One may well ask: if things are so difficult and expensive, why bother to move on and try to expand? The answer must always be: to win more people for Christ. To do that, you need always to plan ahead for somewhere to bring them together. In a telling section of one of his church growth manuals, Peter Wagner says: 'Strangulation . . . occurs when the physical facilities can no longer accommodate the people flow. Sanctuary seating space is one of the vulnerable areas for strangulation. *If in any regular service over 80 percent of the seats are taken, the church is already losing potential members.*'[3]

Many 'thriving' churches need to take heed of this and see that growing can be a better sign of life than to have more or less filled the same building for twenty years. To grow may well mean to move house and above are detailed some of the tensions associated with this. None are tensions that cannot be soothed and sorted out; and the result can be a significant advance in the growth of the church.

Fighting for life

One of the things the devil does is try to kill children. Today we know of this through research into Satanist activities. The Bible tells us of the near death of Moses, and of Jesus. When the infant church was born, Saul had this murderous role thrust on him as he went from house to house dragging away the believers. The dragon stands in front of the woman waiting to devour the child (Revelation 12). If you're engaged in a fight during church planting, be encouraged that it's to be expected. Jesus predicted it. Be encouraged also that he said he was the one to build the church, not us, and that as he builds, the gates of hell will not prevail against it. Trouble may come in any or all the above guises as the new church is born, but let God's people look up and rejoice and see that even though in the world we will have trouble, we can cheer up because Jesus has overcome the world. The one vital thing the new church is to do is to look back, see that it is God who brought the work into being, and that if so, he will keep it safe until the storm passes. Don't be surprised at all kinds of trouble, but meet it joyfully, living by faith in God.

We now move on to a more thorough examination of how to engage in this spiritual fight.

13

Fighting the principalities and powers

From the crafts and assaults of the devil . . .
Good Lord, deliver us.

Prayer Book Litany

A holy church is an awful weapon in the hand of God.

C H Spurgeon

It is my belief . . . that the modern world, and especially the history of the present century, can only be understood in terms of the unusual activity of the devil and the 'principalities and powers' of darkness . . .

In a world of collapsing institutions, moral chaos, and increasing violence, never was it more important to trace the hand of 'the prince of the power of the air', and then, not only to learn how to wrestle with him and his forces, but also how to overcome them 'by the blood of the Lamb and the word of our testimony'. If we cannot discern the chief cause of our ills, how can we hope to cure them?

Martyn Lloyd-Jones

When we try to plant a church in some new territory, we are likely to encounter unseen powers. The new church may find it faces a wall of completely impenetrable indifference as it attempts to win people in an area; or it may find outright opposition. This can be focussed on the question of premises. Innumerable problems can occur in the hiring, heating, or holding on to premises essential to the church's life. Or it may be focussed in people who blacken the name of the Christians. It is good not to be dismayed, as Jesus clearly warned us of this when he said, 'If the world hates you, keep in mind that it hated me first,' and, later, he prays to the Father not that his disciples are taken out of the world but 'that you protect them from the evil one.' Opposition is most commonly expressed in blatant indifference to the presence of the new group of Christians. What the team needs to see is that the struggle may be spiritual as they try to take ground for Christ.

Roger Forster, commenting to me on this book, spoke of his longing 'to make sure that every bit of territory throughout the earth is covered with a church that is influencing the whole of a given area and dealing with the territorial spirits in those areas.' This is a reference to Ephesians 3:10: 'His intent was that now, through the church, the manifold wisdom of God should be made known to the rulers and authorities in the heavenly realms.' But what are these 'territorial spirits', and what form should our warfare take?

Fighting for territory

The idea of territorial spirits has been popularised recently with the publication of Frank Peretti's novels *This Present Darkness* and *Piercing the Darkness*. But behind it is a consistent Biblical exegesis of several passages which seem to imply a real, personal demonic army warring against the purposes of Christ and his church. This interpretation takes literally passages in Daniel 10:13 (referring to the 'prince of the Persian kingdom'), Matthew 12:29 (referring to binding the 'strong man') and Revelation 12:4–19 (referring to the devil's angels being hurled down to earth). This implies the existence of a demonic stronghold in each area that the church is called on to overthrow.

A practice stemming from this world view would be that of identifying ruling spirits in a community. This may involve going back in history and seeing where things have gone wrong, perhaps in the church or in the affairs of the neighbourhood. Some enlightening insights into this are found in John Dawson's *Taking our Cities for God*.[1] John talks of God's redemptive purpose for Los Angeles being contained in the very name of the city: 'The Angels', which means 'the messengers'. He sees Los Angeles as now being the centre of the soft porn entertainment industry: a twisting of God's redemptive purposes. The church of God is called to overcome evil with good and to work in precisely the opposite spirit, namely to communicate again the message about Jesus Christ truthfully, in purity and with loving compassion. John's book is careful to discourage developing spiritual maps, and advises that we should not seek knowledge for the sake of knowledge. But his view is that 'Satan has assigned a hierarchy of principalities, powers and rulers of darkness to specific territories on the earth. In this way he has marred the (God given) culture of every people on earth with some of his own characteristics'. His view is that discerning the particular influence over a place is the key to 'binding the strong man' and beginning to see large numbers converted.

Problems of interpretation . . .

There is certainly a tension here with those interpreters who want to be more cautious. At the far end of the scale, there are evangelicals who emphasise that 'the powers that be are ordained by God' and who feel this theology or demonology polarises the church against human institutions which it should instead be helping. But in fact John Dawson's view does not stop the church from helping the institutions at all: it is not against the institutions, but aware of the powers warring to control them and fighting against them.

Another tension comes when deciding how to fight such territorial spirits. John Wimber has expressed his own concern recently:

> I have some problems with the form of spiritual warfare that teaches we are to go into a given location and ask the Lord to give us revelation on the nature of the demonic principality over that specific geographic region. Then we are to begin speaking to it in order to remove it or lessen its influence over that area.
>
> I have less of a problem with the idea that God may give us revelation about the nature of a demonic principality over a specific geographic region. My major problem here is I cannot find a New Testament example for this procedure.
>
> I have a much greater problem with speaking to demonic principalities. Not only is there no New Testament example of this, but at least two New Testament passages seem to discourage this. (2 Peter 2:10–12; Jude 8–10).[2]

So John Wimber's major reservation has to do with addressing the powers, rather than engaging in the battle. My own view (shared by Michael Harper in a SOMA newsletter) is that Satan and his powers are not omnipresent or omnipotent, as God is, and if they are not everywhere, they must be somewhere! Lesslie Newbigin writes: 'The principalities and powers are real. They are invisible and we cannot locate them in space. They do not exist as disembodied entities floating above this world, or lurking within it. They meet us as embodied in visible and tangible realities – people, nations and institutions, and they are powerful . . .'[3] We should be cautious about addressing these powers, but use every possible weapon to defeat them: discernment, fighting evil with good, intercession, praise, prayer on the streets and preaching the gospel.

Strategy

Discernment

This may be discernment of spiritual opposition, or it may be an understanding of what the nature of the problem is in a team or a church. Particularly at the beginning, leaders need to keep their eye carefully on the waters ahead, discerning any dangers below the surface. What goes wrong on the surface may be violent and troublesome but finding its roots may need spiritual discernment: a combination of listening to God and listening to others. For example, I know of a new church that experienced violent disagreements amongst some of its members as well as a general malaise, lack of energy and feeling of loss of direction. A couple of chance encounters led leaders to discover that a Satanist group had begun 'circling' the local churches, cursing the leadership and praying and fasting for confusion and division among them. Although our desire is not to get hung up about all this, it is right to be informed. It is important to check carefully what we're told.

This is not to say that every trouble comes from a spiritual opponent. All too often it is the fear and pride and ungodly behaviour of team members that leads to trouble. But spiritual opposition is a part of the picture.

Fighting evil with good

In the example just given of spiritual opposition, division had arisen between church members as a result of these fiery darts. The most helpful thing to do in such a situation is to bring the disagreeing parties together and to get them to fast and pray in the opposite spirit. They should come before God at home and together, to pray for the unity described in John 17 to return to the church. They should seek God for love, his love for Jesus, to be in them for one another. As they do this, they will overcome evil with good, and soon find the shield of faith lifted up to stop any further trouble from without. Prayer is the first of our weapons to use in this spiritual war. And not only prayer against opposition but prayer for others, in intercession.

The weapon of intercession

Today, more than ever, the church is being called to intercession. This need not be a burden but a great privilege. To have access to the Father is a great miracle, and the church is realising more and more the delight of being before the Father. It is true that one day in his beautiful, holy, courts is better than a thousand outside. The church planting team needs to cultivate the art of intercession. This means it needs to worship, to wait and listen, to identify with and repent of the sin of its communities, and to feel the burden of pain of Jesus the intercessor. Then, following the model of prayer meetings in Acts, there is a need to pray for boldness to preach the gospel with signs and wonders: 'Now, Lord . . . enable your servants to speak your word with great boldness. Stretch out your hand to heal and perform miraculous signs and wonders through the name of your holy servant Jesus' (Acts 4:29,30). This is not primarily a prayer for others to be converted but for the Christians to become strong to proclaim the message boldly; it is the kind of warring prayer that is needed.

One church that is planting congregations near us is led by Tony Higton. He writes of how intercession has developed at Emmanuel Hawkwell:

> We find that many churches are keen to go forward but they're not really praying very much. They're so busy counselling, praising and going to the latest conference that prayer gets crowded out. At best perhaps a half hour of prayer is added on to a mid-week fellowship or housegroup. Even when a church starts to have intercession meetings or prayer cells they often get torpedoed by personal needs and turn in on themselves.
>
> The nation is not going to be won without intensive intercession and spiritual warfare. The old 'world-tour' prayer meetings are little good. They flit from subject to

subject without tuning in to what God is saying and what He wants praying about. We have twenty-three weekly prayer cells in Hawkwell and also a rule that personal needs are not prayed for in them. Such needs are dealt with elsewhere, for example in the housegroups. Instead, the prayer cells listen to God and then are involved in disciplined, persistent intercession and spiritual warfare. All we do is conceived, born and bred in prayer, partly because we know that that is the only way to extend God's Kingdom.

The weapon of praise

Of course intercession flows from praise, and praise gives rise to intercession. It is worth noting here the power of praise in spiritual warfare. The Bible teaches (Psalm 8) that it stops the whispering of the demonic accuser:

From the lips of children and infants
  You have ordained praise,
because of your enemies
  To silence the foe and the avenger.

The Bible records some breakthroughs that come as a result of praise. One of the best known is reported in 2 Chronicles 20:22. 'As they began to sing and praise, the LORD set ambushes against the men of Ammon and Moab and Mount Seir who were invading Judah, and they were defeated.' No human weapon was used by God's people in their battle, but as they praised God singing, 'Give thanks to the LORD for his love endures forever,' the battle was won by supernatural means. When Moses took the people of Israel through the wilderness, the tribe of Judah led the way. 'Judah' means 'praise'. For Paul and Silas, bruised and bleeding in the Philippian jail, it was as they went on worshipping God until midnight that there was a supernatural intervention in the form of an earthquake – an event which led to the conversion of the jailer and his household and a significant breakthrough for the kingdom of God.

It is this combination of an observation of the effects of

praise in the Bible, plus some convictions about spiritual warfare, which led Graham Kendrick to write his 'Make Way' series. This has helped to motivate hundreds of thousands of Christians to take to the streets of Britain in carnival atmosphere to sing and shout their praises of God.

Make way for the new church

It was shortly after moving to London to be based at Ichthus that Graham produced the first 'Make Way' set of songs and it is fair to say that the concept had its roots in church planting. As Ichthus begin to plant a new congregation one of their first activities will be to gather the Christians to march joyfully through the area targeted for the new church. In his 'Make Way' manual, Graham writes:

> One offensive weapon is the Word of God, and as we take it on our lips and sing or speak it out in faith by the power of the Holy Spirit, the powers of darkness will have to make way for the King of kings!
>
> 'Make Way' is an attempt to provide a resource of songs which are suitable for use to this end. I have tried to focus on many of the truths which are the 'cutting edge' of this sword, and create the kind of songs which both declare vigorously and celebrate joyfully the truth which has set us free. Though the term 'carnival' does have some frivolous and inappropriate connotations, I feel that it nevertheless carries a sense of fun, laughter, colour and music which we need as we confront the gloom, fear and depression around us.[4]

Prayer walks

A practice linked to praise marches is the prayer walk. This is simply and obviously a way of focussing our prayers as we walk the streets of our neighbourhood. The new church will do well to use all means of prayer and this is one of them. I trace a breakthrough in our own community church back to a prayer walk. Furthermore, I recently heard of a community where the great problem was with the local school. The Christians were at a loss as to how to gain a hearing for Christ and resorted to walking round the school in prayer . . . within weeks, a teacher in the school had come to Christ and in turn had brought a colleague to church.

The gospel – our divinely powerful weapon

The greatest weapon in the fight is, of course, telling others about Jesus. Let me return to Paul's famous saying:

> Though we walk in the flesh, we do not war according to the flesh, for the weapons of our warfare are not of the flesh but divinely powerful for the destruction of fortresses. We are destroying speculations and every lofty thing raised up against the knowledge of God and we are taking every thought captive to the obedience of Christ. (2 Corinthians 10:3–5 NASB).

Destroying speculations . . . taking every thought captive

It is likely that Paul knew that as he preached about Jesus Christ and the good news of the escape from judgment that he brings, something happened in the minds of his listeners. That something was that thought became captive to the love of Jesus; speculations about false gods were destroyed by the revelation of the Lord . . . through the preaching of the gospel.

In my view it is likely that as we preach the gospel today we are also addressing the powers of darkness. If they are listening, they will not enjoy being reminded of the public spectacle made of them in the triumph of the cross and resurrection of Jesus Christ.

It is important to note what Paul writes about his time in Ephesus and what Luke reports of Paul's activity in this home of the great temple to Diana. In Acts we read of some dramatic miracles and a tremendous revival as people bound up in the occult repent and burn their books. One might think that Ephesus would be a place where the believers were reported as first identifying and binding the spirits.

But instead what we see is Paul assembling his team and seeing them filled with the Holy Spirit (Acts 19:1–7). He then enters the synagogue and speaks, reasons and persuades. Thrown out of the synogogue, he hires the lecture hall of Tyrannus and again the weapon he uses is to 'reason daily' about the kingdom of God. It is not a question of either prayer or preaching: both are needed. Paul may have fought a battle in prayer that is not recorded. Certainly he prayed for the Ephesians themselves to be filled to overflowing with the knowledge of God and the knowledge of the gospel. But we see from what is recorded in Acts that the church planting team need to be equipped to preach and to gossip the gospel. As they use this divine weapon they will pull down strongholds of unbelief. This is no doubt partly why Paul said to the Roman Christians:

> I am . . . eager to preach the gospel also to you who are in Rome. I am not ashamed of the gospel because it is the power of God for the salvation of everyone who believes . . .

The church planter needs to be gripped by a conviction about the power of the gospel. The team need to be taught the gospel, trained to communicate it. They need to be filled with the Holy Spirit like the team at Ephesus. Then they need to go about using this weapon and seeing how the spiritual opposition shrinks back.

14

Heart cry for revival

Having no righteousness of their own to renounce, they were glad to hear of Jesus who was a friend to publicans and came not to call the righteous but sinners to repentance. The first discovery of their being affected was the sight of the white gutters made by their tears which fell plentifully down their black cheeks as they came out of the coal-pits . . . Sometimes when twenty thousand people were before me, I had not in my own apprehension a word to say either to God or them. But I was never totally deserted . . . The open heavens above me, the prospect of the adjacent fields with the sight of thousands, some in coaches, some on horseback, and some in the trees and at all times affected and in tears was almost too much for me, and quite overcame me.

George Whitefield describing the eighteenth-century revival in England

It is easier to speak about revival than to set about it.

Horatius Bonar

In China, according to the most restrained estimates, two new churches a day are being formed. This is because that suffering church is being visited by revival. How we long for an awakening in our land. Our church is no doubt similar to hundreds in this longing. Six years ago, we taught a mid-week series on the subject. Four years ago we organised a houseparty: its theme? revival. Two years ago we devoted our evening services over a period of months to promoting prayer for revival. Revival has still not yet come. Yet we do not give up looking up and seeking God's face.

We see the desperate state of our culture where violence, rape and suicide rates are continually increasing and homelessness has almost become accepted. According to the latest Mori poll, only 49% of people now believe in life after death. We hang our heads in shame as unrighteous laws are passed and as our football supporters are deported from other European countries like so much radioactive waste.

Yet there are signs of life: the darkness gets darker but the light, where it's shining, is brighter by contrast. For example: CARE is campaigning in parliament; AIDS sufferers are being comforted (see the work of ACET, for example) often by Christians; denominationalism is dying as tens of thousands take to the streets to pray for the nation and engage in interdenominational ventures on both a local and a national scale. And churches are being planted . . . and so my final reason for planting churches is to prepare for revival.

Lyndon Bowring of CARE Trust says:

> I believe that revival is in the air and the people are going to come to know God in our large industrial estates, in our high rise blocks, in the affluent areas. My prayer and desire is that as they come to know Jesus they won't have to go far to find a likeminded group of people with whom they can worship.

Preparing for revival involves prayer, repentance, greater unity and zeal for the gospel. It involves asking God to purge the church of all unholiness and being prepared to face the consequences. But preparing for revival also means planting churches, as a preparation for what we believe is coming from the mercy of God to our country. I conclude with a sample of what just a few Christian leaders are saying about this.

> God's purposes are through the church and through the body of believers, and so you have got to plant churches. So I think it is going to be fundamental that we plant literally hundreds and thousands of new churches (Graham Kendrick).

> We need masses and masses of local churches through which the kingdom of God can come. That is the most effective means of taking the good news of that kingdom throughout the whole of the world (Roger Forster).

> There are many estates, there are many people, where there is no church to minister to them. And I believe that we need to be thinking of planting literally thousands of communities of believers (Roy Pointer).

> I am convinced that Church Planting is a mark of vigorous and outgoing Christianity and is a sign of hope for the future (George Carey).

Let us prepare for revival by all possible means. And as we 'occupy' until he comes, let us be occupied in planning to salt and saturate every single area with more Christ-centred, Holy Spirit filled, good news preaching churches as we join in with what the Holy Spirit is doing in our land today. And may all this be to his pleasure and for his honour.

> That the Lamb who was slain might receive a reward for his suffering . . .

Appendix: A community survey questionnaire

Aims of the survey

1. To gain a deeper understanding of the nature of the area – strengths, weaknesses, neighbourliness, social centres, etc.

2. To gain a clearer understanding of individual and community 'felt' needs, rather than relying on our assumptions.

3. To raise the profile of the church as a caring group of people who want Christianity to be relevant and practical.

Using the survey

You should introduce yourself (if the people do not recognise you) preferably by name and say you are from your congregation.

Ask the person if you could have a few minutes of their time to help with the survey. (It should not take more than five minutes – unless you get talking to them.)

Explain that as a church you are concerned to find out what people think about the area and its needs, including their own personal needs. This is so that the church can be actively involved in serving the community and in making a positive contribution to it.

Community survey

1. (a) Do your work locally?
At home _____ Within 2 miles _____ Further _____
(b) Does your partner work locally?
At home _____ Within 2 miles _____ Further _____

2. How long have you lived in this area?
Under 1 year _____ 1–5 years _____ 6–10 years _____
Longer _____

3. Would you and your neighbours visit one another?
Several times a week _____ Occasionally _____
Rarely _____ Never _____

4. What sort of neighbourhood is this?
Friendly _____ Unfriendly _____
Secure _____ Unsafe _____
Peaceful _____ Violent _____

---

5. What do you see as the best thing about living in this area?

---

6. What do you see as the main problem in this area?

---

7. What facilities do you think are lacking in this area? (Eg leisure services, help with difficulties, services for different age groups, bus service, help for the unemployed, nurseries, etc)

---

8. Do you feel you have people to turn to in a crisis? If 'Yes', who?
Doctor _____ Church _____ A neighbour _____
Family member _____ Friend _____ Other _____

9. Where would you recommend someone to go locally if they needed advice on:
(a) housing
(b) health
(c) legal problems
(d) spiritual problems
(e) financial problems
(f) problems with their kids
(g) coping with loneliness

---

10. If you had questions about things like life after death, the meaning of your life, etc, to whom would you talk?

---

11. Do you attend church?
Regularly _____ Rarely _____ Never _____

12. What would you like to see the church do locally?

13. What do you think of the church in general?

14. Would you like to be kept in touch with future activities of your local church?

Respondent details
Do not ask these questions. Enter the information if it crops up in the conversation.
Address:

Name of respondent: Sex: M F
Age: Under 21 _____ 21–45 _____ 45–65 _____
Over 65 _____
Name of partner:
Number of children:
Names and ages:
Occupation:

Notes

Chapter 1
Introductory quotation from T S Eliot's *Little Gidding* 5
1. In *How to Plant Churches*, Monica Hill (Ed.), MARC, 1984

Chapter 2
Introductory quotation from George Herbert's *The Church Porch*
1. In *How to Plant Churches*, Monica Hill (Ed.), MARC, 1984
2. In *Ten New Churches*, Roger Forster (Ed.), MARC, 1986
3. *Dawn 2000*, Jim Montgomery, William Carey Library, 1989

Chapter 3
Introductory quotation from Dante's *Paradiso*

Chapter 4
Introductory quotation from David Watson's *I Believe in the Church*, Hodder and Stoughton, 1982
1. *Discipling the Nations*, Floyd McClung, YWAM, Amsterdam, 1990

Chapter 5
1. Data from an article by Bob Jackson in *Church of England Newspaper* January 26 1990

Chapter 6
Introductory quotation from Thomas à Kempis' *Of the Imitation of Christ*
1. *Studies in the Sermon on the Mount* (Volume 2), Martyn Lloyd-Jones, IVP, 1976

Chapter 7
Introductory quotations from Milton's *The Passion* and from AW Tozer in *Gathered Gold*, John Blanchard (Ed.), Evangelical Press, 1984
1. *Outline Studies in Acts*, Griffiths Thomas, Eerdmans, 1956
2. *Liturgy and Liberty*, John Leach, Marc, 1989

Chapter 8
Introductory quotation from Campbell McAlpine's *The Practice of Biblical Meditation*, Marshall, Morgan and Scott, 1981
1. *Prophecy: Exercising the Prophetic Gifts of the Spirit Today*, Bruce Yocum, Servant, 1976
2. *School for Prophecy*, six audio tapes by John Wimber, Mercy Publishing, 1988
3. *Lectures to my Students*, C H Spurgeon, Marshall, Morgan and Scott, 1973

Chapter 9
Introductory quotation from Dame Julian's *Revelations of Divine Love*
1. *Equipping the Saints*, Ken Wilson, Vineyard Ministries International
2. *Clearing Away the Rubbish*, Adrian Plass, Minstrel, 1988
3. *The Different Drum*, M. Scott Peck, Arrow Books, 1990

Chapter 10
Introductory quotation from Dante's *Divina Commedia*
1. *Love, Acceptance and Forgiveness*, Jerry Cook, Regal Books, 1979
2. *There's another kind of famine* by John Clarke and Philip Glassborow is copyright © 1988 Thankyou Music
3. *Fear No Evil*, David Watson, Hodder and Stoughton, 1984
4. *Why Revival Tarries*, Leonard Ravenhill, STL, 1972

Chapter 11
Introductory quotation by Dietrich Bonhoeffer is from the *Hodder Book of Christian Quotations*, Tony Castle (Ed.), Hodder and Stoughton, 1982
1. *The Masterplan of Evangelism*, R E Coleman, Revell
2. *Come Holy Spirit*, David Pytches, Hodder and Stoughton, 1985

Chapter 12

Introductory quotation from T S Eliot's *The Hollow Men*

1. *How to Plant Churches*, Monica Hill, MARC, 1984
2. *Ten New Churches*, Roger Forster (Ed.), MARC, 1986
3. *Leading Your Church to Growth*, Peter Wagner, MARC, 1984

Chapter 13

Introductory quotation from C H Spurgeon's *Lectures to my Students* and Martyn Lloyd-Jones' *Christian Warfare*, Banner of Truth, 1976

1. *Taking our Cities for God*, John Dawson, Creation House, 1989
2. *Prophecy*, Seminar by John Wimber, Mercy Publishing, 1990
3. *The Gospel in a Pluralist Society*, Lesslie Newbigin, SPCK, 1989
4. *Make Way Manual*, Graham Kendrick, Kingsway, 1986

Chapter 14

Introductory quotations from George Whitefield's *Journals* and Horatius Bonar, cited in *Gathered Gold*, John Blanchard (Ed.), Evangelical Press, 1984